CALIFORNIA POST EXAM GUIDE (PELLETB)
POST ENTRY-LEVEL LAW ENFORCEMENT TEST BATTERY

Prepare for Success!

Angelo Tropea

ISBN-13: 978-1541348349
ISBN-10: 1541348346

Published by Angelo Tropea

Please note that the passages, examples and questions used in this book are for study purposes only and do **NOT** reflect official names, codes, policy, rules or procedures of any governmental or public or private agency or department.

Unless otherwise clearly indicated, any similarity of names of persons, addresses, places and telephone numbers used in this book to any actual names of persons, addresses and telephone numbers is purely coincidental.

CONTENTS

INTRODUCTION 1

This book deals specifically with the types of questions that may be asked on the California POST exam. The aim of this book is to keep it simple and focused on the PELLETB written exam, instead of complicating it with other information about police officer jobs, tests and benefits in other states which does NOT contribute to attaining a higher score on the California PELLETB exam.

The POST Entry-Level Law Enforcement Test Battery (PELLETB) is a multiple-choice and fill-in-the-blank written examination with questions that measure the writing and reading ability of candidates (language skills).

Although such abilities are usually acquired incrementally over the course of a candidate's school years, there is general agreement that serious preparation utilizing strong study tools such as this book can greatly improve a candidate's chances of doing well.

 **SIMPLE** 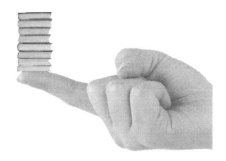 **FOCUSED**

For current information on the test, visit the "Commission on POST" website:

www.post.ca.gov/entry-level-test-battery.aspx

This site provides to law enforcement agencies and job applicants details regarding the POST exam requirements, test-taking, and processing of test results.

The information presented includes an answer to the question, "How do I interpret my results?" The main thing to keep in mind is that you are scored relative to the other candidates. There is no fixed "passing grade." If you score above the average of the other candidates, you are considered to have done well.

Answer sheets are scanned electronically and scores are converted to "T-scores" (a score that places the individual's performance on a bell-curve). A score of 50 is considered average. A score of 40 or below is considered "below average", and a score of 60 or above is considered "above average." Hiring agencies often announce the minimum score that they will consider.

The main thing to keep in mind is that what you need to do is score a little higher than the two persons sitting to your left and to your right.

To help you accomplish this goal, this book provides **exercises and explanations and hints** on the types of questions that may be asked on the written test, thereby helping you to maximize your score and increase your chances of being considered for a job.

A free on-line "Applicant Guide for the Post Entry-Level Law Enforcement Test Battery" is available at:

http://lib.post.ca.gov/publications/poWrittenPracticeTest.pdf

TYPES OF QUESTIONS 2

As per the "Commission on POST" website (www.post.ca.gov/entry-level-test-battery.aspx) the PELLETB test is:
- multiple-choice and fill-in-the-blank written examination
- about 2½ hours long
- with questions on reading and writing ability.

Reading and writing ability are tested with five different types of questions:
1. Spelling
2. Vocabulary
3. Clarity
4. Reading Comprehension
5. Cloze

Reasoning questions may also be included.

Spelling: A sentence is provided with one of the words in the sentence omitted and with a blank ("_____") inserted in place of the omitted word. Four different spellings are provided for the omitted word. The candidate must select the correct spelling of the word.

Vocabulary: Applicants are asked to select the correct meaning of a word from a list of four words.

Clarity: Applicants are presented with a pair of sentences and are asked to select the sentence that is most clearly written.

Reading Comprehension: Applicants are provided with a passage that they must read and then answer questions based on what is stated in the passage.

CLOZE: Candidates are provided with a paragraph where certain words are missing. The candidate must complete the paragraph in a correct and logical manner.

Reasoning: Questions are asked which require the applicant to determine relative values, similarity or differences of items, or the order of letters and numbers.

PREPARING FOR SUCCESS

3

HOW TO PREPARE FOR THE EXAM

After conducting review classes for more than 30 years, I have learned that certain study techniques seem to result in higher marks than do others. However, I have also learned that there are as many study techniques as there are people - and that not all study techniques are appropriate for everyone.

Therefore, I would like to make it clear that what I will be offering are suggestions and not rigid rules. Such factors as the time available for study and the personality, aptitude and resolve of the candidate must all be considered before deciding on how to study. What follows are suggestions that I think will prove helpful.

At the first meeting of a review class, I often ask this question: "Do any of you think that you could win an Olympic race?" Most of the students laugh or shake their heads, especially those who are not in the best physical condition.

I then ask another question: "Do any of you think you could win the race if you were allowed to start running before the gun goes off?"

As the students reflect on this question, I see eyes open wide and smiles spread on many faces. Not cynical smiles, but smiles of hope.

Studying for any exam is in a way similar to preparing and running that Olympic race - except for the fact that you start the race at a moment that you decide.

Some of you may have been excellent students and may be very confident that you will do well on the written test. Others of you may feel less confident.

THE FOLLOWING SUGGESTIONS ARE FOR BOTH OF YOU

For those of you already sharp in the knowledge and skills to take the PELLETB, the study methods that we will discuss will help to sharpen your knowledge even further. And for those of you who have not yet started preparing for the exam, these suggestions will help you to run the race faster so that you will catch up to the lead pack. And for those of you who believe that you are not fast enough, it will give you that head start, that ADVANTAGE that you need to help you near the finish line BEFORE the start gun goes off.

You begin by first convincing yourself that you will succeed! And by bringing into focus the many motivating reasons why you should and WILL succeed!

1) The first consideration in developing a study plan is the length of time from now to the date of the test. A one-month plan, for example, must be different from a longer plan, if only because of the amount of time available.

In a one-month plan we must aim for more intense study periods and the elimination of less-efficient study practices.

2) We must choose wisely the study tools which we are going to use. This book and the "Applicant Preparation Guide for The POST Entry-Level Law Enforcement Test Battery" are a good combination.

The guide is available online at:

http://lib.post.ca.gov/Publications/poWrittenPracticeTest.pdf

3) We must establish and maintain an efficient study schedule, preferably every day for a set amount of time. There is a theory of learning which states that students remember most when they study for short periods instead of one long period. Therefore, seven study periods during the week are more effective than one period during the weekend.

4) Practicing with questions and exams is important because it takes you one step closer to the format and the complexity of the questions which you may find on the actual exam. As you take these quizzes and tests, make note of any questions which you answer incorrectly. Did you answer wrong because you read the question incorrectly or because you need more practice?

If you read the question incorrectly, try to keep in mind the following suggestion: Read every word of the question. This way, you will not skip such important qualifying words as MUST, SHALL, or MAY. These tiny but powerful words can completely change the meaning of a question.

Also, try to spend more time on your weakest areas. Do not concentrate on areas that you are most comfortable with and that you already know.

In summary, please try to remember that your chances of success depend greatly on the time and effort that you put into preparing for the exam. If you really want to succeed, start the race before the gun goes off - and put it in your mind that YOU WILL SUCCEED!

CALIFORNIA POST EXAM GUIDE (PELLETB)

TEST-TAKING SUGGESTIONS

1. The night before the exam, get a good night's sleep! The night before the exam is not the time to go to a party or to a sports game. Scientific studies have shown that sleep deprivation dulls the mind.

2. If possible, try not to cram. If you can, review the exercises, suggestions and hints, and practice tests. If you have been studying correctly, you owe it to yourself to rest. Cramming often hurts instead of helping. Pace yourself each day and you won't feel the need to sprint at the last moment.

3. Pay careful attention to the time and location of the test site. Plan to get there early, in comfort and without having to rush. For more than thirty years I have heard many horror stories of candidates not arriving at the test site on time.

4. Do not go into the test hungry. Eat and drink enough to last you through the test. Keep hydrated.

5. Take with you any required items: pens, pencils, ID, any required forms, or payment, etc.

6. At the test site, listen attentively and don't take anything for granted. Follow directions carefully. Make sure you don't miss any information that might help you get a higher score. Pay close attention on how to mark the answer sheet, especially your answers to the CLOZE questions.

7. Familiarize yourself with the answer sheet. If you have any questions, ask the proctor as soon as possible.

8. Crystallize in your mind how many questions you must answer - and the types of questions.

9. Quickly develop a time budget - and during the exam, check the time on your watch to make sure you are not falling behind. Do not rely on the proctor to keep you informed of the time.

10. Don't spend too much time on any one question (unless you have finished all the other questions and are satisfied with your answers).

11. Read each question carefully. Select the best choice – and try to figure out why each of the other choices is not correct. Every five or so questions, double-check that you are marking the corresponding answer for the question that you are up to.

12. If you find during the test that there are questions for which you believe there is more than one valid answer, do not lose time thinking about it. Select the best answer that you can - and go on.

13. If during the test, you feel tense or nervous, try to stretch your body to relieve the uncomfortable symptoms. If you need to, take a minute to breathe in and out.

14. Don't pay any attention to people leaving before you. Chances are they will not do as well as you.

———————————

SPELLING

4

Question Format

A sentence is provided with one of the words in the sentence omitted. A blank ("_____") is inserted in place of the omitted word. Four different spellings are provided for the omitted word. You must select the choice with the correct spelling of the word.

Suggestions

1. Although the spelling and vocabulary words included in the test are not drawn from a specific word list, the "Applicant Preparation Guide for the Post Entry-Level Law Enforcement Test Battery" states that "…the words that comprise the test are words that could likely find themselves in police reports or in other writing done by officers."

Because of this, we have included in Section 10 a list of selected important words for law enforcement.

2. Try to look at this list briefly every time you study. Looking at the list often and in short sessions will help increase your sensitivity to the correct spelling of these words. You will also retain more than you would in one or two long study sessions. (Also, if there are words that you are unsure of their meaning, take a moment and look up their definitions.)

3. Answer all the spelling questions in this book. This will help you to become more comfortable with the words and the question format. Write your answers on a piece of paper, and not in the book. By doing so, you can retake the tests without being influenced by your prior work.

4. Keep in mind that each candidate is scored relative to the other candidates. You don't have to achieve perfection. All you need to do is score higher than the average of your fellow test-takers.

Consider the following 5 Examples

1. Because the suspect used a dangerous instrument, the charge was elevated to _____
assault.

A. aggrivated

B. aggraveted

C. aggrevated

D. aggravated

The correct spelling is "aggravated." The correct answer is **"D. aggravated."**

Because the suspect used a dangerous instrument, the charge was elevated to **aggravated**
assault.

----

2. To _____ success, one must usually work very hard.

A. acheive

B. achive

C. achieve

D. acheve

The correct spelling is "achieve." The correct answer is **"C. achieve."**

To **achieve** success, one must usually work very hard.

----

3. Because the officer found a pouch with eight ounces of heroin under the driver's car seat,
the driver was charged with _____ of an illegal substance.

A. posession

B. possession

C. possesion

D. possesson

The correct spelling is "possession." The correct answer is **"B. possession."**

Because the officer found a pouch with 8 ounces of heroin under the driver's car seat, the driver was charged with **possession** of an illegal substance.

----

4. An offender who is found guilty of committing three or more felonies at different times is classified as a _____ offender.

A. persistent

B. persistant

C. persestent

D. persestint

The correct spelling is "persistent." The correct answer is **"A. persistent."**

An offender who is found guilty of committing three or more felonies at different times is classified as a **persistent** offender.

----

5. The suspect was identified because he had a skull and bone _____ on the back of his right shoulder.

A. tatoo

B. tattu

C. tattoo

D. tatitu

The correct spelling is "tattoo." The correct answer is "**C. tattoo.**"

The suspect was identified because he had a skull and bone **tattoo** on the back of his right shoulder.

CALIFORNIA POST EXAM GUIDE (PELLETB)

Exercise 1

Instructions: For the following 5 questions, select the choice with the correct spelling of the omitted word in the sentence.

1. The two police raids were conducted _____.
A. simultanously
B. simutaneously
C. simulteneously
D. simultaneously

2. Officer Dan Briskoll was assigned to _____ of the suspected drug house.
A. survellance
B. surveillance
C. survelliance
D. surveliance

3. The Sergeant did not _____ that the officer patrol the neighborhood without a partner.
A. recomend
B. reccommend
C. reccomend
D. recommend

4. The suspect admitted that he _____ used drugs.
A. occassionally
B. occasionaly
C. occasionally
D. ocassionaly

5. The informer said he could _____ that the suspect would be at the bar on Monday night.
A. garentee
B. garantee
C. garanty
D. guarantee

Answers 1-5

1. D. simultaneously

The two police raids were conducted **simultaneously**.

2. B. surveillance

Officer Dan Briskoll was assigned to **surveillance** of the suspected drug house.

3. D. recommend

The Sergeant did not **recommend** that the officer patrol the neighborhood without a partner.

4. C. occasionally

The suspect admitted that he **occasionally** used drugs.

5. D. guarantee

The informer said he could **guarantee** that the suspect would be at the bar on Monday night.

_____

Exercise 2

Instructions: For the following 5 questions, select the choice with the correct spelling of the omitted word in the sentence.

1. The Captain said that he will _____ attend the community meeting.

A. deffinitely

B. definitely

C. definately

D. definitly

2. He voluntarily confessed that he _____ the burglary.

A. comitted

B. commited

C. committed

D. comited

3. The youth stated that he had an _____ to the Red Sword gang.

A. allegience

B. alegiance

C. allegiance

D. allegaince

4. The doctor emphasized that it would not be _____ to question the suspect until he was fully conscious.

A. advizable

B. adviseable

C. adviseble

D. advisable

5. The witness stated that the alleged perpetrator was not a friend, but only an _____.

A. acquaintance

B. aquaintance

C. acquaintence

D. acquaintenence

Answers 1-5

1. B. definitely

   The Captain said that he will **definitely** attend the community meeting.

2. C. committed

   He voluntarily confessed that he **committed** the burglary.

3. C. allegiance

   The youth stated that he had an **allegiance** to the Red Sword gang.

4. D. advisable

   The doctor emphasized that it would not be **advisable** to question the suspect until he was fully conscious.

5. A. acquaintance

The witness stated that the alleged perpetrator was not a friend, but only an **acquaintance**.

———————————

Exercise 3

Instructions: **For the following 10 questions, select the choice with the correct spelling of the omitted word in the sentence.**

1. The evidence indicated that the burglary had been committed by an _____.

A. amatuer

B. amatur

C. amateur

D. amature

2. After a complete investigation, the detective could not discover any _____ motive for the willful damage to the auto.

A. apparent

B. apparrent

C. aparent

D. aparrent

3. The police officer on patrol told the young couple that it was not _____ to stroll through the park after sunset.

A. adviseable

B. advizabel

C. adviceable

D. advisable

4. The _____ of the gang leader greatly decreased the amount of neighborhood violence.

A. absense

B. absence

C. absennse

D. absance

5. The officer was instructed to wear his bio-hazard _____.

A. equiptment

B. ecquipment

C. eqipment

D. equipment

6. The motorist stated that he did not _____ the speed limit.

A. esceed

B. exceed

C. xceed

D. exeede

7. The victim told the officer that she was _____ for his quick response.

A. grateful

B, gratful

C. gratefull

D. gratfull

8. The bicycle thief was about six feet in _____.

A. heigth

B. hight

C. height

D. hieght

9. The three witnesses all gave different times for the _____.

A. occurence

B. occurrance

C. occurrence

D. ocurrance

10. All the persons in the bank at the time of the robbery were asked to fill-out a _____.

A. questionnair

B. questionaire

C. questionnare

D. questionnaire

Answers 1-10

1. C. amateur

   The evidence indicated that the burglary had been committed by an **amateur**.

2. A.apparent

   After a complete investigation, the detective could not discover any **apparent** motive for the willful damage to the auto.

3. D. advisable

   The police officer on patrol told the young couple that it was not **advisable** to stroll through the park after sunset.

4. B. absence

   The **absence** of the gang leader greatly decreased the amount of neighborhood violence.

5. D. equipment

   The officer was instructed to wear his bio-hazard **equipment**.

6. B. exceed

   The motorist stated that he did not **exceed** the speed limit.

7. A. grateful

   The victim told the officer that she was **grateful** for his quick response.

8. C. height

   The bicycle thief was about six feet in **height**.

9. C. occurrence

   The three witnesses all gave different times for the **occurrence**.

10. D. questionnaire

　　All the persons in the bank at the time of the robbery were asked to fill-out a **questionnaire**.

Exercise 4

Instructions: For the following 15 questions, select the choice with the correct spelling of the omitted word in the sentence.

1. The unprovoked attack was _____ by all of the victims.

A. unforsen

B. unforseen

C. unforeseen

D. unforsene

2. Officer Jane Bryant 's _____ for the day included a visit to the elementary school.

A. schedull

B. skedule

C. sckedul

D. schedule

3. When the officer arrived on the scene, he _____ performed CPR on the heart attack victim.

A. imediately

B. immediately

C. immediatly

D. imediatly

4. The squad car is in good working order because it receives periodic _____ .

A. maintainance

B. maintenance

C. maintenence

D. mantenence

5. Fortunately, the bruise on the victim's face was barely _____.

A. noticeable

B. noticable

C. notiseable

D. noteceable

6. Because of his actions, he was charged with _____.

A. harasment

B. harrasment

C. harrassment

D. harassment

7. To help prevent illness, parents are responsible for providing their children with proper

_____.

A. hygene

B. hygine

C. hygeine

D. hygiene

8. The suspect tried to _____ by hiding in the attic.

A. dissappear

B. dissapear

C. disappear

D. disappere

9. The teenagers vandalized seven headstones in the Fairmont _____.

A. cemetery

B. cemetary

C. cemmetary

D. cemmetery

10. The active shooter was wearing a _____ suit.

A. camoflage

B. camoflague

C. camuflage

D. camouflage

11. The emergency 911 call was received from the _____ .

A. neighbor

B. neihbor

C. neighbur

D. neihbour

12. Because of the unaccounted firearms, it was _____ to pat down all the people in the room.

A. neccessary

B. necesary

C. necessary

D. necassery

13. The officer asked the witness if he knew what _____ the physical fight.

A. preceeded

B. preceded

C. precceded

D. precedid

14. Because of the active shooter warning, all the _____ in the office sheltered in place.

A. personell

B. personnel

C. personel

D. perssonell

15. Because they found a firearm under his jacket, he was charged with illegal _____ of a firearm.

A. posession

B. possesion

C. posesion

D. possession

CALIFORNIA POST EXAM GUIDE (PELLETB)

Answers 1-15

1. C. unforeseen

   The unprovoked attack was **unforeseen** by all of the victims.

2. D. schedule

   Officer Jane Bryant 's **schedule** for the day included a visit to the elementary school.

3. B. immediately

   When the officer arrived on the scene, he **immediately** performed CPR on the heart attack victim.

4. B. maintenance

   The squad car is in good working order because it receives periodic **maintenance**.

5. A. noticeable

   Fortunately, the bruise on the victim's face was barely **noticeable**.

6. D. harassment

   Because of his actions, he was charged with **harassment**.

7. D. hygiene

   To help prevent illness, parents are responsible for providing their children with proper **hygiene**.

8. C. disappear

   The suspect tried to **disappear** by hiding in the attic.

9. A. cemetery

   The teenagers vandalized seven headstones in the Fairmont **cemetery**.

10. D. camouflage

    The active shooter was wearing a **camouflage** suit.

11. A. neighbor

The emergency 911 call was received from the **neighbor**.

12. C. necessary

Because of the unaccounted firearms, it was **necessary** to pat down all the people in the room.

13. B. preceded

The officer asked the witness if he knew what **preceded** the physical fight.

14. B. personnel

Because of the active shooter warning, all the **personnel** in the office sheltered in place.

15. D. possession

Because they found a firearm under his jacket, he was charged with illegal **possession** of a firearm.

VOCABULARY 5

Question Format

A sentence is provided with one of the words in the sentence underlined. You must select among four choices the one with the most accurate synonym or definition of the word.

Suggestion: After you select the answer, read the sentence with the word that you selected, making sure that the word conforms to the meaning expressed by the sentence.

Examples 1-5

Instructions: For each of the following 5 sentences, choose the word that is closest in meaning to the underlined word in the sentence.

1. The officer admonished the teenager for littering in the park.

A. extolled

B. touted

C. lauded

D. reprimanded

2. The suspect confessed that his intention had been to damage the car adjacent to the one that actually got damaged.

A. away

B. farthest

C. closest

D. distant

3. When Officer Jenkins arrived at the scene, he was apprised of the situation by Officer Fenmore who had witnessed the incident.

A. misinformed

B. misled

C. informed

D. deceived

4. The suspect was handcuffed because he acted in a <u>belligerent</u> manner.

A. pacific

B. combative

C. uncontentious

D. peaceful

5. The party was <u>boisterous</u>, so the neighbor complained to the police.

A. noisy

B. sedate

C. quiet

D. noiseless

Answers 1 - 5

1. **D. reprimanded** (Admonished is similar to reprimanded, rebuked, scolded,)

2. **C. closest** (Adjacent and closest both mean abutting, neighboring, or flanking.)
    (Away, farthest, and distant indicate "far away" from the car.)

3. **C. informed** (Apprised and informed both mean being told about something.)
    (Misinformed, misled, and deceived are contrary to the meaning of informed.)

4. **B. combative** (Pacific, uncontentious, and peaceful are nonaggressive ways to act, the
    opposite of combative.)

5. **A. noisy** (Sedate, quiet, and noiseless all express calmness, the opposite of boisterous.)

_____

CALIFORNIA POST EXAM GUIDE (PELLETB)

Exercise 1

Instructions: For each of the following 5 sentences, choose the word that is closest in meaning to the underlined word in the sentence.

1. After a long trial, the defendant was <u>exonerated</u>.

A. condemned

B. sentenced

C. acquitted

D. convicted

2. He considered the public remark to be a <u>defamation</u> of his character.

A. commendation

B. approval

C. disparagement

D. commendation

3. The suspect denied that he was <u>enamored</u> with the complainant.

A. embittered

B. repulsed

C. soured

D. enchanted

4. The gang member had a reputation as being a <u>formidable</u> enemy.

A. powerful

B. weak

C. easy

D. feeble

5. He remained overnight in the hospital because the <u>laceration</u> was serious.

A. sunburn

B. gash

C. irritation

D. medication

Answers 1-5

1. **C. acquitted** (Acquitted is similar to exonerated, absolved, vindicated.)

2. **C. disparagement** (Disparagement is similar to defamation, smear, denigration.)

3. **D. enchanted** (Enchanted is similar to enamored, captivated, enraptured.)

4. **A. powerful** (Powerful is similar to formidable, tough, tremendous.)

5. **B. gash** (Gash is similar to laceration, slash.)

———————

Exercise 2

Instructions: For each of the following 5 sentences, choose the word that is closest in meaning to the underlined word in the sentence.

1. After considering all the facts, the officer concluded that the negligent party was the driver of the Toyota.
A. attentive
B. thoughtful
C. native
D. careless

2. At the scene he discovered a prodigious amount of evidence.
A. insignificant
B. unremarkable
C. tremendous
D. small

3. As soon as he stopped using drugs, he repudiated the gang and all its rules.
A. disavowed
B. accepted
C. enforced
D. approved

4. Based on the facts, the motive was <u>unequivocal</u>.

A. ambiguous

B. apparent

C. unclear

D. vague

5. All the equipment made the emergency back-pack <u>cumbersome</u>.

A. compact

B. burdensome

C. convenient

D. graceful

Answers 1-5

1. **D. careless** (Careless is similar to negligent, irresponsible, reckless.)

2. **C. tremendous** (Tremendous is similar to colossal, vast, massive.)

3. **A. disavowed** (Disavowed is similar to abandoned, dismissed, disclaimed.)

4. **B. apparent** (Apparent is similar to unequivocal, clear-cut, indisputable.)

5. **B. burdensome** (Burdensome is similar to cumbersome, inconvenient, unwieldy.)

Exercise 3

Instructions: For each of the following 10 sentences, choose the word that is closest in meaning to the underlined word in the sentence.

1. He complained that because of his skinny body, he was the subject of <u>derision</u> by all the other classmates.

A. mockery

B. admiration

C. approval

D. praise

2. The possibility of being discovered and punished was the major <u>deterrent</u> to committing the crime.

A. assistance

B. encouragement

C. disincentive

D. incentive

3. Although it was clear he committed the crime, the motive remained an <u>enigma</u> until the first day of trial.

A. certainty

B. mystery

C. clearness

D. apparency

4. Although the charge was serious, his answers were <u>flippant</u>.

A. serious

B. courteous

C. respectful

D. frivolous

5. Fueled by his alcohol consumption, his tears were <u>incessant</u>.

A. intermittent

B. unending

C. interrupted

D. broken

6. He gained the trust of the donators by appearing to be a <u>benevolent</u> person.

A. cruel

B. caring

C. miserly

D. malevolent

7. Although he stated that he was not involved in the fight, the suspect looked <u>disheveled</u>.

A. clean

B. neat

C. unwrinkled

D. ruffled

8. Because he transferred the funds under false pretense, he was charged with <u>embezzlement</u>.

A. negligence

B. incompetence

C. blunder

D. larceny

9. He made the threat in an effort to <u>extort</u> a large sum of money from the bank.

A. offer

B. give

C. coerce

D. surrender

10. He was easily duped by the offer because he was <u>illiterate</u>.

A. intelligent

B. uneducated

C. learned

D. able

Answers 1-10

1. **A. mockery** (Mockery is similar to derision, ridicule, disparagement.)

2. **C. disincentive** (Disincentive is similar to deterrent, discouragement, preventive.)

3. **B. mystery** (Mystery is similar to enigma, puzzle, stumper.)

4. **D. frivolous** (Frivolous is similar to flippant, flighty, impertinent.)

5. **B. unending** (Unending is similar to incessant, endless, unrelenting.)

6. **B. caring** (Caring is similar to benevolent, benign, compassionate.)

7. **D. ruffled** (Ruffled is similar to disheveled, tousled, messed up.)

8. **D. larceny** (Larceny is similar to embezzlement, misappropriation, theft.)

9. **C. coerce** (Coerce is similar to extort, extract, wrench.)

10. **B. uneducated** (Uneducated is similar to illiterate, uninstructed, unschooled.)

Exercise 4

Instructions: For each of the following 15 sentences, choose the word that is closest in meaning to the underlined word in the sentence.

1. The main reason why he got himself into trouble was that he was young and <u>impetuous</u>.

A. cautious

B. impulsive

C. calm

D. considerate

2. For the first few minutes after he gained consciousness, he was <u>incoherent</u>.

A. connected

B. intelligible

C. understandable

D. incomprehensible

3. He had an <u>irrational</u> fear of riding in a car.

A. responsible

B. logical

C. sensible

D. unreasonable

4. The handle of the hammer was <u>protruding</u> from the car's side door.

A. shrinking

B. extending

C. contracting

D. depressing

5. He saw the silhouette of the suspect in front of the wall.

A. brightness

B. contour

C. light

D. brilliance

6. He used the instrument to siphon gas from the gas tank.

A. drain

B. restore

C. return

D. restitute

7. The drugs were being processed by ABZ Labs and its subsidiary.

A. opponent

B. headquarters

C. branch

D. enemy

8. When we pulled him out of the rubble, his complexion was pallid.

A. healthy

B. hearty

C. strong

D. pale

9. She had no recollection of the train entering the danger zone.

A. vagueness

B. reason

C. memory

D. purpose

10. Restitution is often ordered in juvenile delinquency cases.

A. reimbursement

B. dissatisfaction

C. imprisonment

C. parole

11. The heavy and bulky bomb gear was a <u>hindrance</u> to the special officer.

A. aid

B. handicap

C. assistance

D. benefit

12. The drink made her very <u>lethargic</u>.

A. active

B. drowsy

C. alert

D. animated

13. The use of drugs was <u>prevalent</u> in the Bordmore District.

A. common

B. exceptional

C. scarce

D. limited

14. The attorney made a motion to <u>suppress</u> the introduction of the evidence.

A. allow

B. permit

C. sanction

D. repress

15. The empty building was <u>vandalized</u> by three teenagers.

A. mended

B. repaired

C. fixed

D. damaged

Answers 1-15

1. **B. impulsive** (Impulsive is similar to hasty, hurried, precipitant.)

2. **D. incomprehensible** (Incomprehensible is similar to incongruous, inarticulate, rambling.)

3. **D. unreasonable** (Unreasonable is similar to nonsensical, reasonless, illogical.)

4. **B. extending** (Extending is similar to protruding, extruding, butting out.)

5. **B. contour** (Contour is similar to silhouette, shape, form.)

6. **A. drain** (Drain is similar to pump, funnel, extract.)

7. **C. branch** (Branch is similar to subsidiary, partner company, auxiliary company.)

8. **D. pale** (Pale is similar to pallid, ashen, grey.)

9. **C. memory** (Memory is similar to recollection, recall, knowledge.)

10. **A. reimbursement** (Reimbursement is similar to restitution, indemnity, indemnification.)

11. **B. handicap** (Handicap is similar to hindrance, impediment, interference.)

12. **B. drowsy** (Drowsy is similar to lethargic, sleepy, inactive.)

13. **A. common** (Common is similar to prevalent, frequent, rampant.)

14. **D. repress** (Repress is similar to suppress, muzzle, withhold.)

15. **D. damaged** (Damaged is similar to smash, wreck, disfigure.)

CLARITY

6

Clarity questions evaluate your ability to express yourself clearly enough so that others will understand.

Two versions (a and b) of a sentence are provided. You are asked to decide which version is the most clearly and correctly written.

Some of the major reasons why a sentence may be unclear are:

1) modification errors (confusion as to who or what we are trying to describe)

2) unclear references (confusion as to who or what we are referring to, or talking about)

3) run-on sentences (two or more sentences not properly separated) and

4) sentence fragments (incomplete, partial sentences)

Even without studying a thick book of grammer rules (with countless "exceptions" to the general rules) you can (by practicing and by repetition) become more sensitive to sentence (clarity) errors and spot them quickly.

When answering sentence "CLARITY" questions, try to keep in mind the following brief rules:

1. Is the sentence in a logical order? Are the main ideas properly connected?
Example: Which of the following three choices is/are correct?
 (1) The boy who dropped out of high school didn't like to study.
 (2) The boy didn't like to study dropped out of high school.
 (3) The boy dropped out didn't like to study.
Answer: (1) is the most logical and grammatically correct.

2. Every sentence begins with a capital letter and ends with a period.

3. For a sentence to be complete, it must have at minimum a subject and a predicate. Otherwise, it is just a sentence fragment.

A **subject** is usually a noun (person, place, or thing) about which something is asked or stated.
Example: The police officer (subject) speaks softly.

A **predicate** contains a verb (an "action" word) and is the part of the sentence about what is said about the subject. In the above example, the predicate is "speaks."

4. A comma usually goes before the following words: but, for, or, nor, so, yet – when the word connects two main clauses.
Examples:
He didn't like to study, but he liked to play.
He scored a high mark, for he had received good training.
You can try hard and succeed, or you can make a feeble attempt and fail.
He didn't try hard, nor did he try for long.
He studied long and hard, so he passed.
He was sick when he took the test, yet he did very well.

5. A comma usually goes after an introductory phrase.
Examples:
When you study, you build up the neural connections in your brain.
Because of hard work and a little good luck, he succeeded in life.

6. A comma usually goes between separate items in a list or series of adjectives.
Examples:
The boy was young, proud, and happy.
The tall, young, proud officer walked up to the front of the room.

7. Commas usually set-off parenthetical elements.
Examples:
Young boys, <u>as Abraham Lincoln once observed</u>, should not be afraid to work hard.
American soldiers, <u>generally speaking,</u> are very well trained.

8. A semicolon is usually used between main clauses (with similar, related content) not linked by: but, for, or, nor, so, yet.
Examples:
The young boys played basketball; the older men sat on the bleachers.
The war had many battles; few were as fierce as this one.

Notice that the first letter after the semicolon is NOT capitalized.

9. The colon is usually used to direct attention to a series (a list).
Example: The ingredients of success are as follows: hard work, commitment, and luck.
(Notice here also that the first letter after the colon is NOT capitalized.)

———————————

<u>Examples of modification errors</u>
<u>(adjectives placed in the wrong part of the sentence)</u>

Modifiers are words or phrases that describe other words or phrases.

Misplaced modifiers are simply modifiers which due to their incorrect placement in the sentence, make the sentence confusing.

- **Aware of the dangers of the dark alley, Officer Smith's gun was always in the ready position.**

A careful reading highlights the defect in the sentence. The way the sentence is written, it seems to say that <u>Officer Smith's gun</u> (and not Officer Smith) was aware of the dangers of the dark alley.

The following is a clearer version:
Because Officer Smith was aware of the dangers of the alley, he always held his gun in the ready position.

- **Trying to find cover from the bullets, the truck offered the best alternative.**

This sentence incorrectly states that the truck was trying to find cover from the bullets.

The following is a clearer version:
Trying to find cover from the bullets, <u>the officer</u> decided that the truck offered the best alternative.

- **Barking loudly because he located the heroin, Officer Jane Henson gave the police dog a biscuit.**

This sentence states that Officer Jane Henson was barking loudly.

The following is a clearer version:
Because the dog had located the heroin and was barking loudly, Officer Jane Henson gave him a biscuit.

- **Because he was busy, he decided to prepare every two days the report.**

This sentence is clumsy. The location in the sentence of the "every two days" phrase interrupts the flow of the sentence.

The following is a clearer and smoother version:
Because he was busy, he decided to prepare the report every two days.

- **The captain selected officers who were well-groomed in the parade.**

Clearer and smoother: The captain selected well-groomed officers for the parade.

- **The officer was surprised to stumble on the diamond woman's watch they had been searching for.**

Clearer version: The officer was surprised to stumble on the woman's diamond watch they had been searching for.

- **By dutifully patrolling his area, the gang members would realize that the officer was a professional.**

Clearer version: As a result of the officer dutifully patrolling his area, the gang members realized that the officer was a professional.

- **Jumping between the two rooftops, I spotted the suspect.**

Clearer version: I spotted the suspect as he was jumping between two rooftops.

- **The officer polished the silver tiny firearm that he was given as a reward.**

Clearer version: The officer polished the tiny silver firearm that he was given as a reward.

- **Running into the wooded area, I spotted the suspect.**

Clearer version: I spotted the suspect running into the wooded area.

Examples of reference errors
(confusion regarding who or what we are talking about)

- **The Police Officer asked him to help him pick out the suspect in his case.**

Whose case are we referring to? The Police Officer's case or the person's case?

(The "his" in "his case" is ambiguous. It doesn't tell us whose case we are referring to.)

Clearer version (if the case is the Police Officer's case):
The Police Officer asked him to help him pick out the suspect in the Police Officer's case.

Clearer version (if the case is the person's case):
The Police Officer asked him to help pick out the suspect in the person's case.

- **After the suspect butted heads with the other driver, his head started bleeding.**

Whose head started bleeding – the suspect, or the other driver?

(The "his" in "his head" is ambiguous. It does not make clear whose head started bleeding.)

Clearer version (if the bleeding head is that of the suspect):
After the suspect butted heads with the other driver, the suspect's head started bleeding.

Clearer version (if the bleeding head is that of the other driver):

After the suspect butted heads with the other driver, the other driver's head started bleeding.

• **Both Officer Wanda Traynor and Officer Barbara Gomez loved her pet Chihuahua.**

Who is the owner of the pet Chihuahua – Officer Traynor or Officer Gomez?

(The "her" in "her pet Chihuahua" does not make clear who owns the dog.)

Clearer version (if Officer Wanda Traynor is the owner):
Both Officer Wanda Traynor and Officer Barbara Gomez loved Officer Traynor's pet Chihuahua.

Clearer version (if Officer Barbara Gomez is the owner):
Both Officer Wanda Traynor and Officer Barbara Gomez loved Officer Gomez's pet Chihuahua.

• **After hiding the Ming vase in the antique chest, the art dealer sold it to a wealthy art collector.**

What was sold – the Ming vase, the antique chest, or both the vase and the chest?

Clearer version (if only the Ming vase was sold):
After hiding the Ming vase in the antique chest, the art dealer sold the vase to a wealthy art collector.

Clearer version (if only the antique chest was sold):
After hiding the Ming vase in the antique chest, the art dealer sold the chest to a wealthy art collector.

Clearer version (if both the Ming vase and the antique chest were sold):
After hiding the Ming vase in the antique chest, the art dealer sold both the chest and the Ming vase to a wealthy art collector.

• **Step number nine is to remove the handle from the manual starter and repair it.**

What has to be repaired – the handle, the manual starter, or both?

Clearer version (if only the handle has to be repaired):
Step number nine is to remove the handle from the manual starter and repair the handle.

Clearer version (if only the manual starter has to be repaired):
Step number nine is to remove the handle from the manual starter and repair the manual starter.

Clearer version (if both the manual starter and the handle have to be repaired):

Step number nine is to remove the handle from the manual starter and then repair both the handle and the manual starter.

• **The Captain and the Sergeant explained to the special riot squad that the mayor would hold them accountable if his rules of engagement were not followed.**

Who is the "<u>them</u>" in the phrase "would hold <u>them</u> accountable" – the Captain and the Sergeant, the special riot squad, or both the Captain and the Sergeant and the special riot squad?

Clearer version (if only the Captain and the Sergeant would be held accountable):
The Captain and the Sergeant explained to the special riot squad that the mayor would hold the Captain and the Sergeant accountable if his rules of engagement were not followed.

Clearer version (if only the special riot squad would be held accountable):
The Captain and the Sergeant explained to the special riot squad that the mayor would hold the squad accountable if his rules of engagement were not followed.

Clearer version (if the Captain, the Sergeant, and the special riot squad would be held accountable):
The Captain and the Sergeant explained to the special riot squad that the mayor would hold the Captain, the Sergeant, and the squad accountable if his rules of engagement were not followed.

• **Officer Brown skipped the squad meeting, which turned out to be a big mistake.**

What does the "which" in the phrase "<u>which</u> turned out" refer to – the squad meeting, or the officer skipping the meeting?

Clearer version (if only the meeting was a big mistake):
The meeting, which turned out to be a big mistake, was skipped by Officer Brown.

Clearer version (if skipping the meeting was a big mistake):
Officer Brown's skipping the squad meeting turned out to be a big mistake.

• **The patrol manual did not contain the rule, but we followed it anyway.**

What does the "<u>it</u>" in the phrase "followed <u>it</u> anyway" refer to – the rule or the manual?

Clearer version (if the "it" refers to the rule):
The patrol manual did not contain the rule, but we followed the rule anyway.

Clearer version (if the "it" refers to the manual):
The patrol manual did not contain the rule, but we followed the manual anyway.

- **Officer Kerns asked the maintenance person to clean up his mess.**

To whom is "<u>his</u>" in the phrase "his mess" refer to – Officer Kerns, or the maintenance person?

Clearer version (if "his" refers to the maintenance person):
Officer Kerns asked the maintenance person to clean up the mess that the maintenance person made.

Clearer version (if "his" refers to Officer Kearns):
Officer Kerns asked the maintenance person to clean up the mess that Officer Kearns made.

- **Every time Officer Chin visits the store owner, he gives him a big hello.**

To whom does the "<u>he</u>" in the phrase "he gives him" refer to – Officer Chin, or the store owner?

Clearer version (if "he" refers to Officer Chin):
Every time Officer Chin visits the store owner, he gives the store owner a big hello.

Clearer version (if "he" refers to the store owner):
Every time Officer Chin visits the store owner, the store owner gives him a big hello.

<u>Examples of run-on sentences</u>
<u>(Two or more sentences not properly connected)</u>

The following is an example of two complete sentences:
Sentence 1: The witness arrived at the courthouse at eleven o'clock in the morning.
Sentence 2: He was accompanied by an officer assigned to ensure his safety.

The two separate sentences are clear and grammatically correct.

The following is an example of a run-on sentence:
The witness arrived at the courthouse at eleven o'clock in the morning, he was accompanied by an officer assigned to ensure his safety.

The following are examples of sentences that combine the two sentences in a grammatically correct manner:
1. Accompanied by an officer assigned to secure his safety, the witness arrived at the courthouse at eleven o'clock in the morning.

2. The witness and an officer assigned to secure his safety arrived at the courthouse at eleven o'clock in the morning.

When reviewing possible run-on sentences, keep in mind that two sentences may be joined and NOT become a run-on sentence IF they are joined properly, as in the following examples:

1. If there is a close relationship between two sentences, they may be joined by a semicolon, as in the following example:

The witness arrived at the courthouse at eleven o'clock in the morning; he was accompanied by an officer assigned to ensure his safety.

Note that the first letter of the first word after the semicolon is <u>NOT</u> capitalized.

2. If the second sentence contains a list of items, a colon may be used, as in the following example:

Sentence 1: The delivery van was filled with office supplies.
Sentence 2: The supplies were log books, pencils, pens, and memo pads.

The delivery van was filled with office supplies: log books, pencils, pens, and memo pads.

Note that the first letter of the first word after the semicolon is <u>NOT</u> capitalized.

3. Another method of joining two sentences is by using an introductory phrase (referred academically by such names as subordinating conjunctions).

Sentence 1: The sergeant listed the steps to be taken.
Sentence 2: He told all the recruits to practice the steps.

After the sergeant listed the steps to be taken, he told all the recruits to practice the steps.

<u>Sentence fragments</u>

Sentence fragments are <u>pieces</u> of a sentence, but not a complete sentence that contains both a subject (noun) and a predicate (verb).

A NOUN is the name of a person, place, or thing: hat, car, Sacramento, George Washington, mountain, etc.

A VERB is a word that expresses action: walk, talk, run, smile, wink, think, etc. (or a "state of being" such as is, was, etc.)

FOR A SENTENCE TO BE COMPLETE, IT MUST HAVE AT MINIMUM A SUBJECT AND A PREDICATE. <u>OTHERWISE, IT IS JUST A SENTENCE FRAGMENT.</u>

A **subject** is usually a <u>noun</u> about which something is asked or stated.

A **predicate** contains a <u>verb</u> and is the part of the sentence about what is said about the subject. In the above example, the predicate is "speaks."

Example of a complete sentence

The police officer who just transferred to this precinct (subject) speaks (predicate) in a very calm voice.

Examples of sentence fragments

1. The police officer who just transferred.
(The predicate – the VERB – is missing. What did the person who just transferred do or say?)

2. Speaks in a very calm voice.
(The SUBJECT – the person who speaks – is missing.)

3. Increased the number of hours reserved for sensitivity classes.
(The SUBJECT is missing. Who increased the hours?)

In short, sentence fragments leave you stranded with only a part of the complete thought.

For the following 10 examples, choose whether the example is a sentence (A) or a sentence fragment (B).

1. When the police officer arrived.
A. sentence
B. sentence fragment

Answer: B. sentence fragment (The "police officer" is a noun and the subject of the phrase. However, there is no VERB (no action word). The fragment does not tell us what the officer did when he arrived.)

-----

2. The victim ran away from the attacker.
A. sentence
B. sentence fragment

Answer A. sentence (The sentence expresses a complete thought. It has both a subject and a predicate. The subject of the sentence (the victim) and (ran) a verb that is the predicate of the sentence.)

-----

3. On days when he was assigned to the Coliseum.
A. sentence
B. sentence fragment

Answer B. sentence fragment (There is a subject "he", but no verb that tells us what happened or what he did on the days that he was assigned to the coliseum.)

-----

4. When it was raining.
A. sentence
B. sentence fragment

Answer B. sentence fragment ("When it was raining" is the subject. There is no verb (action word) that tells us what happened when it was raining. It is an incomplete thought.)

-----

5. Officers who have completed the six-month course.
A. sentence
B. sentence fragment

Answer B. sentence fragment (There is no verb (no predicate). The fragment is only a partial, incomplete thought.)

-----

6. The area where the suspect fled to.
A. sentence
B. sentence fragment

Answer B. sentence fragment (Again, there is no verb (no predicate) to tell anything about the area where the subject fled to.)

-----

7. Because he frequents bars in the neighborhood.
A. sentence
B. sentence fragment

Answer B. sentence fragment (There is no verb (predicate.))

-----

8. Walking to the scene of the crime.
A. sentence
B. sentence fragment

Answer B. sentence fragment (There is no subject. Who was walking?)

-----

9. A short, stocky male in his fifties.
A. sentence
B. sentence fragment

Answer B. sentence fragment (There is no verb (predicate). What about the short, stocky man in his fifties?)

-----

10. One of the first things to remember.
A. sentence
B. sentence fragment

Answer B. sentence fragment (There is no verb (predicate). What about one of the first things to remember?)

_____

For the following 10 examples, choose whether the example is a sentence (A) or a sentence fragment (B).

1. A wide range of opinions, all radical.
A. sentence
B. sentence fragment

-----

2. The dark corner where the broom was.
A. sentence
B. sentence fragment

-----

3. He was vomiting the drugs he had just swallowed.
A. sentence
B. sentence fragment

-----

4. Deciding quickly not to follow.
A. sentence
B. sentence fragment

-----

5. Clutching the gun, I ran to the other end of the warehouse.
A. sentence
B. sentence fragment

-----

6. The same as the other box in the middle of the warehouse.
A. sentence
B. sentence fragment

-----

7. Especially when you are not sure, you hesitate before acting.
A. sentence
B. sentence fragment

-----

8. The same, except for the color of the room.
A. sentence
B. sentence fragment

-----

9. The wind parted the curtains.
A. sentence
B. sentence fragment

-----

10. With the officer next to me.
A. sentence
B. sentence fragment

Answers 1-10
1. B. sentence fragment
2. B. sentence fragment
3. A. sentence
4. B. sentence fragment
5. A. sentence
6. B sentence fragment
7. A. sentence
8. B. sentence fragment
9. A. sentence
10. B. sentence fragment

Questions 1-5

Instructions: For the following 5 questions, decide which sentence is most clearly written.
Choose "A" if sentence "a" is clearer than sentence "b".
Choose "B" if sentence "b" is clearer than sentence "a".

Question 1:
a. The park is sometimes strewn with litter, but they still manage to have fun.
b. The children have fun in the park, even though it is strewn with litter.

Question 2:
a. The store owner hit the burglar with a broom when he entered the back room.
b. When the burglar entered the back room, the store owner hit him with a broom.

Question 3:
a. The lady was terrified of dogs and cats.
b. Terrified both of dogs and cats.

Question 4:
a. The evidence was placed in duffle bags by the evidence squad.
b. The evidence was placed by the evidence squad in duffle bags.

Question 5:
a. He decided to go with a police dog, one who had experience with that warehouse.
b. He decided to go with a police dog. One that had experience with that warehouse.

Answers 1-5

Answer 1. B (Choice "a" is not correct because it is not clear who "they" refers to.)

Answer 2. B (Choice "a" is not correct because it is not clear who "he" refers to.)

Answer 3: A (Choice "b" is a sentence fragment. It states that someone is terrified of both dogs and cats, but does not explain who is terrified.)

Answer 4: A (Choice "b" makes it sound like the evidence squad was in the duffle bags.)

Answer 5: A (Choice "b" is not correct because the second part is a sentence fragment.)

Questions 1-10

Instructions: For the following 10 questions, decide which sentence is most clearly written.
Choose "A" if sentence "a" is clearer than sentence "b".
Choose "B" if sentence "b" is clearer than sentence "a".

Question 1:

a. Fully aware of the possible danger, his adrenalin activated.

b. Fully aware of the possible danger, he felt his adrenalin activating.

Question 2:

a. The squad covered all the territory, even the furthest areas.

b. Even the furthest areas. The squad covered all the territory.

Question 3:

a. The store owner told his employee to help him search for his missing box.

b. The store owner told his employee to help search for the store owner's missing box.

Question 4:

a. Aided by the four bystanders, the officer was able to subdue the robber.

b. The officer was able to subdue the robber. Aided by the four bystanders.

Question 5:

a. The recruits patrolled the eastern section, the veterans patrolled the western section.

b. The recruits patrolled the eastern section. The veterans patrolled the western section.

Question 6:

a. Trying not to get drenched, the canopy offered good shelter.

b. Trying not to get drenched, the officer sheltered under the canopy.

Question 7:

a. While wearing all their gear, the officers searched all day and night.

b. The officers searched all day and night. Wearing all their gear.

Question 8:

a. After the driver and the pedestrian fought, the driver's cheek started bleeding.

b. After the driver fought with the pedestrian, his cheek started bleeding.

Question 9:

a. The firearm was more than ten years old. It needed to be replaced.

b. The firearm was more than ten years old, it needed to be replaced.

Question 10:

a. Creaking loudly every time it opened, Officer Jacobs oiled his squad room door.

b. Officer Jacobs oiled his squad room door because it was creaking loudly every time it opened.

Answers 1-10

Answer 1: B (Sentence "a" states that the adrenalin was fully aware - and not the person, as in "b".)

Answer 2: A ("b" contains the sentence fragment, "Even the furthest areas.")

Answer 3: B ("a" is confusing because it is not clear whose box is missing. The "his" in "his missing box" does not make it clear whose box is missing.)

Answer 4: A ("b" contains the sentence fragment, "Aided by the four bystanders.")

Answer 5: B ("a" is a run-on sentence. It should be expressed in two sentences, as in "b".)

Answer 6: B ("a" contains a modification error. It makes it seem like the canopy was trying not to get drenched.)

Answer 7: A ("b" contains the sentence fragment. "Wearing all their gear.")

Answer 8: A ("b" contains a reference error. Who is "his" referring to - the driver or the pedestrian?)

Answer 9: A ("b" is a run-on sentence.)

Answer 10: B ("a" has a modification error. The "creaking" is modifying Officer Jacobs.)

Questions 1-15

Instructions: For the following 15 questions, decide which sentence is most clearly written.
Choose "A" if sentence "a" is clearer than sentence "b".
Choose "B" if sentence "b" is clearer than sentence "a".

Question 1:

a. Both Officer Robert Lerner and Officer David Osweld took a ride on his motorcycle.

b. Both Officer Robert Lerner and Officer David Osweld took a ride on Officer Lerner's motorcycle.

Question 2:

a. The training was long and difficult, especially the ten-mile run.

b. The training was long and difficult. Especially the ten-mile run.

Question 3:

a. Because the abandoned buildings were filthy, he shampooed every day his hair.

b. Because the abandoned buildings were filthy, he shampooed his hair every day.

Question 4:

a. He tapped his foot impatiently. Waiting for the lawyer to arrive.

b. While waiting for the lawyer to arrive, he tapped his foot impatiently

-----

Question 5:

a. After hiding the drug vial in the teddy bear, he took it to his contact.

b. After hiding the drug vial in the teddy bear, he took the teddy bear to his contact.

Question 6:

a. The suspect was questioned in room seven, surprisingly, he cooperated.

b. The suspect surprisingly cooperated when he was questioned in room seven.

Question 7:

a. The victim selected the person who looked like the attacker in the lineup.

b. The victim selected the person in the lineup who looked like the attacker.

Question 8:

a. The officer told the motorist to take the card out of the wallet and hold it in the air.

b. The officer told the motorist to take the card out of the wallet and hold the card up in the air.

Question 9:

a. The students escaped from the back door. The teachers followed.

b. The students escaped from the back door, the teachers followed.

Question 10:

a. The officer noticed the leather man's wallet that was reported stolen.

b. The officer noticed the man's leather wallet that was reported stolen.

Question 11:

a. The officers took the toys to the children's hospital, where they were very much appreciated.

b. The toys to the children's hospital. Very much appreciated.

Question 12:

a. The witness threw out the paper, which was a mistake.

b. The witness made the mistake of throwing out the paper.

Question 13:

a. The cars were parked on the sidewalk. The vans were parked in the parking lot.

b. The cars were parked on the sidewalk, the vans were parked in the parking lot.

Question 14:

a. By patrolling his assigned area with a police dog, the gang members realized he was serious about stopping crime.

b. By patrolling his assigned area with a police dog, the police officer made it clear to gang members that he was serious about stopping crime.

Question 15:

a. The witness showed the officer the gold dirty bracelet she had found on the ground.

b. The witness showed the officer the dirty gold bracelet she had found on the ground.

Answers 1-15

Answer 1: B ("a" contains a reference error. The "his" in "<u>his</u> motorcycle" does not make clear who owns the motorcycle.)

Answer 2: A ("b" contains the sentence fragment, "Especially the ten-mile run.")

Answer 3: B ("a" is clumsy. The arrangement of the phrase "shampooed every day his hair" interrupts the flow of the sentence.)

Answer 4: B ("a" contains the sentence fragment, "Waiting for the lawyer to arrive.")

Answer 5: B ("a" has a reference error. It does not make clear what specifically was the primary object that was intended to be taken to the contact.)

Answer 6: B ("a" is a run-on sentence.)

Answer 7: B ("b" is smoother and does not have the modification error that "a" has.)

Answer 8: B ("a" has a reference error. It does not make clear what should be held up in the air.)

Answer 9: A ("b" is a run-on sentence.)

Answer 10: B ("a" has a modification error. The correct version of "leather man's wallet" is "man's leather wallet.")

Answer 11: A ("b" has the sentence fragment, "Very much appreciated." The fragment contains the verb "appreciated", but it does not state what was appreciated.)

Answer 12: B ("a" contains a reference error. "Which was a mistake" does not make clear what was a mistake: the witness throwing out the paper OR the paper itself?)

Answer 13: A ("b" is a run-on sentence.)

Answer 14: B ("a" has a modification error. Sentence "a" is confusing as to who is patrolling with the dog - the gang members or the police officer?)

Answer 15: B ("a" has a misplaced modifier. A "dirty gold bracelet" is clearer than " gold dirty bracelet.")

Instructions: For the following 15 questions, decide which sentence is most clearly written.
Choose "A" if sentence "a" is clearer than sentence "b".
Choose "B" if sentence "b" is clearer than sentence "a".

Question 1:

a. Both Officer Franken and Officer Solomon practiced with his firearm.

b. Both Officer Franken and Officer Solomon practiced with Officer Solomon's firearms.

Question 2:

a. While wearing all their gas masks, the officers broke into the drug house.

b. The officers broke into the drug house. Wearing their gas masks.

Question 3:

a. The shoppers escaped from the side entrance. The workers followed.

b. The shoppers escaped from the side entrance, the workers followed.

Question 4:

a. Trying to avoid the Molotov cocktail, the bus shelter offered a good shield.

b. Trying to avoid the Molotov cocktail, the officer used the bus shelter as a shield.

Question 5:

a. With the help of a passing motorist, the officer succeeded in pulling the driver out of the burning car.

b. The officer succeeded in pulling the driver out of the burning car. With the help of a passing motorist

-----

Question 6:

a. The store owners set up stalls on the sidewalk, the police vans were parked by the curb.

b. The store owners set up stalls on the sidewalk. The police vans were parked by the curb.

Question 7:

a. Trying to collect the parade streamers, the oversized bags proved very useful.

b. While trying to collect the parade streamers, the officers realized that the oversized bags were very useful.

Question 8:

a. The petitions were scattered in front of the political office. The signs were piled in front of the main entrance.

b. The petitions were scattered in front of the political office, the signs were piled in front of the main entrance.

Question 9:

a. Because of the determined demeanor, the judge realized which attorney would prove to be the most persistent.

b. Because of the determined demeanor of Counselor Waring, the judge realized which attorney would prove to be the most persistent.

Question 10:

a. The passenger spotted a silver small phone on the floor of the taxi.

b. The passenger spotted a small silver phone on the floor of the taxi.

Question 11:

a. Seeing the anarchist running away from the Purple Party member, the officer felt relieved.

b. The officer felt relieved. Seeing the anarchist running away from the Purple Party member.

Question 12:

a. Even the young children realized who the person with the mask was.

b. They realized who the person with the mask was. Even the young children.)

Question 13:

a. The bank manager thanked the sergeant for finding his report.

b. The bank manager thanked the sergeant for finding the bank manager's report.

Question 14:

a. Aided by the residents of the neighborhood, the officer was able to cut the crime rate in half.

b. The officer was able to cut the crime rate in half. Aided by the residents of the neighborhood.

Question 15:

a. The officer put the medical instrument in the first aid box and told the rookie to take it to the van.

b. The officer put the medical instrument in the first aid box and told the rookie to take the first aid box to the van.

Answers 1- 15

Question 1:

a. Both Officer Franken and Officer Solomon practiced with his firearm.

b. Both Officer Franken and Officer Solomon practiced with Officer Solomon's firearms.

Answer 1: B ("a" contains a reference error. The "his" in "<u>his</u> firearm" does not make clear who owns the firearm.)

Question 2:

a. While wearing all their gas masks, the officers broke into the drug house.

b. The officers broke into the drug house. Wearing their gas masks.

Answer 2: A ("b" contains a sentence fragment, "Wearing their gas masks.")

Question 3:

a. The shoppers escaped from the side entrance. The workers followed.

b. The shoppers escaped from the side entrance, the workers followed.

Answer 3: A ("b" is a run-on sentence.)

Question 4:

a. Trying to avoid the Molotov cocktail, the bus shelter offered a good shield.

b. Trying to avoid the Molotov cocktail, the officer used the bus shelter as a shield.

Answer 4: B ("a" contains a modification error. It makes it seem like the bus shelter was trying to avoid the Molotov cocktail.)

Question 5:

a. With the help of a passing motorist, the officer succeeded in pulling the driver out of the burning car.

b. The officer succeeded in pulling the driver out of the burning car. With the help of a passing motorist

Answer 5: A ("b" contains the sentence fragment, "With the help of a passing motorist.")

Question 6:

a. The store owners set up stalls on the sidewalk, the police vans were parked by the curb.

b. The store owners set up stalls on the sidewalk. The police vans were parked by the curb.

Answer 6: B ("a" is a run-on sentence.)

Question 7:

a. Trying to collect the parade streamers, the oversized bags proved very useful.

b. While trying to collect the parade streamers, the officers realized that the oversized bags were very useful.

Answer 7: B ("a" contains a modification error. It makes it seem like the oversized bags were trying to collect the streamers.)

Question 8:

a. The petitions were scattered in front of the political office. The signs were piled in front of the main entrance.

b. The petitions were scattered in front of the political office, the signs were piled in front of the main entrance.

Answer 8: A ("b" is a run-on sentence.)

Question 9:

a. Because of the determined demeanor, the judge realized which attorney would prove to be the most persistent.

b. Because of the determined demeanor of Counselor Waring, the judge realized which attorney would prove to be the most persistent.

Answer 9: B ("a" has a modification error. Sentence "a" is confusing as to whose demeanor we are talking about.)

Question 10:

a. The passenger spotted a silver small phone on the floor of the taxi.

b. The passenger spotted a small silver phone on the floor of the taxi.

Answer 10: B ("a" has a misplaced modifier. A "small silver phone" is smoother and clearer than a silver small phone.")

Question 11:

a. Seeing the anarchist running away from the Purple Party member, the officer felt relieved.

b. The officer felt relieved. Seeing the anarchist running away from the Purple Party member.

Answer 11: A ("b" contains the sentence fragment, "Seeing the anarchist running away from the Purple Party member.")

Question 12:

a. Even the young children realized who the person with the mask was.

b. They realized who the person with the mask was. Even the young children.)

Answer 12: A ("b" contains a sentence fragment, ""Even the young children.")

Question 13:

a. The bank manager thanked the sergeant for finding his report.

b. The bank manager thanked the sergeant for finding the bank manager's report.

Answer 13: B ("a" is confusing because it is not clear whose report was missing.)

Question 14:

a. Aided by the residents of the neighborhood, the officer was able to cut the crime rate in half.

b. The officer was able to cut the crime rate in half. Aided by the residents of the neighborhood.

Answer 14: A ("b" contains the sentence fragment, "Aided by the residents of the neighborhood.")

Question 15:

a. The officer put the medical instrument in the first aid box and told the rookie to take it to the van.

b. The officer put the medical instrument in the first aid box and told the rookie to take the first aid box to the van.

Answer 15: B ("a" has a reference error. It does not state clearly what the rookie should take to the van.)

READING COMPREHENSION

7

These questions evaluate your ability to understand written passages, especially **details** in sentences and paragraphs. The passages may vary from one paragraph to one page in length.

SUGGESTION

Pay careful attention to the **details** of the four answer choices (A, B, C and D).

Match every detail of each choice to the detail in the written comprehension passage.

The correct answer choice will be the **only** choice that matches **all** the details correctly.

(To double-check your answer, make sure that each of the other choices is not correct because it contains at least one detail that does **not** match what is stated in the sentences or paragraphs.)

CALIFORNIA POST EXAM GUIDE (PELLETB)

The following is an example of a READING COMPREHENSION QUESTION:

Example 1 Question

The overtime policy for California Police Officers must be uniform and applied fairly in all cases. First, the decision to work overtime is not at the discretion of police officers. It may be mandated when necessary and other suitable volunteer officers are not available to perform the work during the overtime period. Although certain duties may be performed by any police department employees in any job title, some duties must be performed only by officers in designated ranks or who have successfully completed required training. An example of this may be found in the preparation of Monthly Statistical Reports. These reports may only be prepared by California Police Officers who have more than five years' experience as a California Police Officer and who have completed the required statistical training course.

1. Which of the following statements is best supported by the preceding paragraph?

A. All police department employees may prepare Monthly Statistical Reports.

B. All police department employees must prepare Monthly Statistical Reports.

C. Monthly Statistical Reports may be prepared by all employees who have completed the required statistical training course.

D. None of the above

Example 1 Answer

1. Which of the following statements is best supported by the preceding paragraph?

A. All police department employees may prepare Monthly Statistical Reports.

B. All police department employees must prepare Monthly Statistical Reports.

C. Monthly Statistical Reports may be prepared by all employees who have completed the required statistical training course.

D. none of the above (Correct answer)

"A" is not correct because Monthly Statistical Reports may be prepared **only** by California Police Officers who have completed the required statistical training course **and** who have five years' experience.

"B" is not correct because only California Police Officers who are qualified may prepare the statistical reports.

"C" is not correct because in addition to completing the required statistical training course, California Police Officers must **ALSO** have five years' experience.

"D" is the answer because it correctly states that "A", "B," and "C" are all incorrect.

Example 2 Question

A famous person once said that in discussions among persons, what often has the greatest impact is what is left unsaid. A polite reminder and a firm and balanced glance from a California Police Officer sometimes has more effect than a loud rebuke concerning the incorrect display of a car registration form. The "glance" or "look," however, has little effect when not supported by a professional and determined appearance. California Police Officers should therefore be well groomed and always be in clean and appropriate uniform.

2. According to the above passage, which of the following statements is correct?

A. California Police Officers should never speak loudly.

B. California Police Officers should always wear all the parts of their uniform.

C. California Police Officers should not look at persons if they are not in appropriate uniform.

D. Appearance is important in performing some of the duties of a California Police Officer.

Example 2 Answer

According to the above passage, which of the following statements is correct?

A. California Police Officers should never speak loudly.

(**THIS IS NOT CORRECT**. The passage deals with not speaking loudly **at the time of discussing an incorrectly displayed car registration form** and NOT at any other time, including an emergency when a loud alert may be required to avoid injury.)

B. California Police Officers should always wear all the parts of their uniform.

(**THIS IS NOT CORRECT**. The passage states, "California Police Officers should therefore be well groomed and always be in clean and **appropriate** uniform." The uniform of a California Police Officer differs according to the season. California Police Officers are not required to wear their winter garments in summer.)

C. California Police Officers should not look at persons if they are not in appropriate uniform.

(**THIS IS NOT CORRECT**. This passage deals with the way California Police Officers look at persons at the time of discussing an incorrect display of a car registration form and recommends proper "glances" or "looks" at other times, but it does not recommend that California Police Officers not look at people when they are not in appropriate uniform.)

D. Appearance is important when performing some of the duties of a California Police Officer.

(**THIS IS THE CORRECT CHOICE. The main emphasis of the passage is the importance of a "professional and determined appearance."**)

Example 3 Question

Properly preparing reports is an important part of a California Police Officer's duties. This is especially true when filling out incident reports for "aided" cases or "unusual occurrences." An "Aided" report is used when a California Police Officer assists a California State employee or a member of the public who has been injured and requires emergency or medical assistance. "Unusual Occurrence" reports are prepared for other types of incidents, including discovery of weapons or illegal substances. In addition to providing a paper trail for legal and liability reasons, these reports are a valuable resource when reviewing staffing, procedures, work performance, and planning.

3. According to the above selection:

A. An "Aided" incident report is used to document the discovery of a pouch containing heroin.

B. "Aided" and "Unusual Occurrence" reports prevent lawsuits against California Police Officers.

C. An "Aided" report is filled out if a California Police Officer calls for an ambulance for an injured person.

D. An "Aided" report must be filled out whenever a California Police Officer speaks with a person with disabilities.

Example 3 Answer

3. According to the above selection:

A. An "Aided" incident report is used to document the discovery of a pouch containing heroin.

(**NOT CORRECT**. An "Aided" report is used when a California Police Officer assists a California State employee or a member of the public who was been injured and requires **emergency or medical assistance."**)

B. "Aided" and "Unusual Occurrence" reports prevent lawsuits against California Police Officers.

(**NOT CORRECT**. "In addition to <u>providing a paper trail</u> for legal and liability reasons, these reports are a valuable resource when reviewing staffing, procedures, work performance, and planning." These reports provide a paper trail, but do not prevent lawsuits.)

C. An "Aided" report is filled out if a California Police Officer calls for an ambulance for an injured person.

(**THIS IS THE ANSWER. The statement is correct because the passage states, "An "Aided" report is used when a California Police Officer assists a California State employee or a member of the public who has <u>been injured and requires emergency or medical assistance.</u>"**)

D. An "Aided" report must be filled out whenever a California Police Officer speaks with a person with disabilities.

(**NOT CORRECT**. The Aided Report is used when a California Police Officer provides emergency or medical assistance.)

Answer Question 1 based on the information provided in the following section of PL 120.60.

PL § 120.60 Stalking in the first degree

A person is guilty of stalking in the first degree when he or she commits the crime of stalking in the third degree as defined in subdivision three of section 120.50 or stalking in the second degree as defined in section 120.55 of this article and, in the course and furtherance thereof, he or she:

1. intentionally or recklessly causes physical injury to the victim of such crime, or

2. commits a class A misdemeanor defined in article one hundred thirty of this chapter, or a class E felony defined in section 130.25, 130.40 or 130.85 of this chapter, or a class D felony defined in section 130.30 or 130.45 of this chapter.

Stalking in the first degree is a class D felony.

-----

1. According to the preceding definition of stalking in the first degree, which of the following choices is an example of stalking in the first degree?

A. A male intentionally or recklessly causes physical injury to the victim of any crime.

B. A male or female commits a class A misdemeanor defined in article one hundred thirty of this chapter, or a class E felony defined in section 130.25, 130.40 or 130.85 of this chapter, or a class D felony defined in section 130.30 or 130.45 of this chapter (PL).

C. An adult intentionally or recklessly causes physical injury to the victim of a crime; or commits a class A misdemeanor defined in article one hundred thirty of this chapter, or a class E felony defined in section 130.25, 130.40 or 130.85 of this chapter, or a class D felony defined in section 130.30 or 130.45 of this chapter (PL).

D. none of the above

Answer Question 2 based on the information provided in the following example of a Miranda Warning.

The following is an example of a Miranda Warning:

"You have the right to remain silent when questioned.

Anything you say or do may be used against you in a court of law.

You have the right to consult an attorney before speaking to the police and to have an attorney present during questioning now or in the future.

If you cannot afford an attorney, one will be appointed for you before any questioning, if you wish.

If you decide to answer any questions now, without an attorney present, you will still have the right to stop answering at any time until you talk to an attorney.

Knowing and understanding your rights as I have explained them to you, are you willing to answer my questions without an attorney present?"

-----

2. According to this version of the Miranda Warning, which of the following four choices is incorrect?

A. The person warned must be asked if he/she is willing to answer any questions without an attorney present after the person knows and understands his/her rights as explained.

B. The person must be informed that anything the person says or does may be used against the person in a court of law.

C. If the person cannot afford an attorney, one will be appointed only at the time of trial.

D. A person without an attorney present has the right to stop answering at any time until the person talks to an attorney.

Answer Question 3 based on the information provided in the following section of CPL 720.10.

CPL § 720.10 Youthful offender procedure; definition of terms

As used in this article, the following terms have the following meanings:

1. "Youth" means a person charged with a crime alleged to have been committed when he was at least sixteen years old and less than nineteen years old or a person charged with being a juvenile offender (ages 13, 14 or 15) as defined in subdivision forty-two of section 1.20 of this chapter.

2. "Eligible youth" means a youth who is eligible to be found a youthful offender. Every youth is so eligible unless:

(a) the conviction to be replaced by a youthful offender finding is for (i) a class A-I or class A-II felony, or (ii) an armed felony as defined in subdivision forty-one of section 1.20, except as provided in subdivision three, or (iii) rape in the first degree, criminal sexual act in the first degree, or aggravated sexual abuse, except as provided in subdivision three, or

(b) such youth has previously been convicted and sentenced for a felony, or

(c) such youth has previously been adjudicated a youthful offender following conviction of a felony or has been adjudicated on or after September first, nineteen hundred seventy-eight a juvenile delinquent who committed a designated felony act as defined in the family court act.

-----

3. According to the preceding, which one of the following persons qualifies as an "eligible youth"?

A. Bernard Cranson, male, 20 years old, is arrested and charged with a crime. He was never found to be a juvenile offender.

B. Martin Frieds, male, 20 years old, is arrested and charged with a crime. He has previously been adjudicated a youthful offender following conviction of a felony.

C. Cecilia Norwin, a female, 17 years old, is arrested and charged with a crime. She had previously been adjudicated a youthful offender following a conviction and sentencing for a felony.

D. none of the above

Answers 1 - 3

Answer Question 1 based on the information provided in the following section of PL 120.60.

PL § 120.60 Stalking in the first degree

A person is guilty of stalking in the first degree when he or she commits the crime of stalking in the third degree as defined in subdivision three of section 120.50 or stalking in the second degree as defined in section 120.55 of this article **and, in the course and furtherance thereof, he or she:**

1. intentionally or recklessly causes physical injury to the victim of such crime, or

2. commits a class A misdemeanor defined in article one hundred thirty of this chapter, or a class E felony defined in section 130.25, 130.40 or 130.85 of this chapter, or a class D felony defined in section 130.30 or 130.45 of this chapter.

Stalking in the first degree is a class D felony.

> A couple of careful readings of the preceding section of law can help us to summarize it as follows:
>
> A person is guilty of stalking in the first degree **IF** the person in the process of committing the crime of stalking in the second degree or stalking in the third degree **ALSO** does at least one of the following:
>
> 1. intentionally or recklessly causes physical injury to the victim of the second or third degree stalking, OR
>
> 2. commits one of the specific A misdemeanors or E felonies listed in PL 120.60.
>
> Stalking in the first degree is a class D felony.

1. According to the preceding definition of stalking in the first degree, which of the following choices is an example of stalking in the first degree?

A. A male intentionally or recklessly causes physical injury to the victim of any crime.

(WRONG. According to our summary, the physical injury must be in the course of committing stalking in the second degree or stalking in the third degree and other specified offense.)

B. A male or female commits a class A misdemeanor defined in article one hundred thirty of this chapter, or a class E felony defined in section 130.25, 130.40 or 130.85 of this chapter, or a class D felony defined in section 130.30 or 130.45 of this chapter (PL).

(WRONG. According to our summary, the offense must be in the course of committing stalking in the second degree or stalking in the third degree.)

C. An adult intentionally or recklessly causes physical injury to the victim of a crime; or commits a class A misdemeanor defined in article one hundred thirty of this chapter, or a class E felony defined in section 130.25, 130.40 or 130.85 of this chapter, or a class D felony defined in section 130.30 or 130.45 of this chapter (PL).

(WRONG. According to our summary, the physical injury must be in the course of committing stalking in the second degree or stalking in the third degree.)

D. none of the above

(THIS IS THE RIGHT CHOICE. All the other choices ("A", "B," and "C") do not consider that the physical injury or commission of any of the specified crimes <u>must</u> be during the commission of stalking in the second degree or stalking in the third degree.)

Answer Question 2 based on the information provided in the following example of a Miranda Warning.

The following is an example of a Miranda Warning:

"You have the right to remain silent when questioned.

Anything you say or do may be used against you in a court of law.

You have the right to consult an attorney before speaking to the police and to have an attorney present during questioning now or in the future.

If you cannot afford an attorney, one will be appointed for you before any questioning, if you wish.

If you decide to answer any questions now, without an attorney present, you will still have the right to stop answering at any time until you talk to an attorney.

Knowing and understanding your rights as I have explained them to you, are you willing to answer my questions without an attorney present?"

-----

2. According to this version of the Miranda Warning, which of the following four choices is <u>incorrect?</u>

A. The person warned must be asked if he/she is willing to answer any questions without an attorney present after the person knows and understands his/her rights as explained.

(CORRECT STATEMENT. The last sentence states, "Knowing and understanding your rights as I have explained them to you, are you willing to answer my questions without an attorney present?" Statement "A" is therefore a correct statement and not the incorrect statement that we are looking for.)

B. The person must be informed that anything the person says or does may be used against the person in a court of law.

(CORRECT STATEMENT. Sentence two states, "Anything you say or do may be used against you in a court of law." Statement "B" is therefore a correct statement and not the incorrect statement that we are looking for.)

C. If the person cannot afford an attorney, one will be appointed only at the time of trial.

(INCORRECT STATEMENT. Therefore, "C" is the answer. Sentence four states, "If you cannot afford an attorney, one will be appointed for you <u>before any questioning</u>, if you wish.")

D. A person without an attorney present has the right to stop answering at any time until the person talks to an attorney.

(CORRECT STATEMENT. Sentence five states, "If you decide to answer any questions now, without an attorney present, you will still have the right to stop answering at any time until you talk to an attorney." Statement "D" is therefore a correct statement and not the incorrect statement that we are looking for.)

Answer question 3 based on the information provided in the following section of CPL 720.10.

CPL § 720.10 Youthful offender procedure; definition of terms

As used in this article, the following terms have the following meanings:

1. "Youth" means a person charged with a crime alleged to have been committed when he was at least sixteen years old and less than nineteen years old or a person charged with being a juvenile offender (ages 13, 14 or 15) as defined in subdivision forty-two of section 1.20 of this chapter.

2. "Eligible youth" means a youth who is eligible to be found a youthful offender. Every youth is so eligible unless:

(a) the conviction to be replaced by a youthful offender finding is for (i) a class A-I or class A-II felony, or (ii) an armed felony as defined in subdivision forty-one of section 1.20, except as provided in subdivision three, or (iii) rape in the first degree, criminal sexual act in the first degree, or aggravated sexual abuse, except as provided in subdivision three, or

(b) such youth has previously been convicted and sentenced for a felony, or

(c) such youth has previously been adjudicated a youthful offender following conviction of a felony or has been adjudicated on or after September first, nineteen hundred seventy-eight a juvenile delinquent who committed a designated felony act as defined in the family court act.

-----

3. According to the preceding, which one of the following persons qualifies as an "eligible youth"?

A. Bernard Cranson, male, 20 years old, is arrested and charged with a crime. He was never found to be a juvenile offender.

(DOES NOT QUALIFY. The youth must be less than 19 years old (See "1" in section 720.10)

B. Martin Frieds, male, 20 years old, is arrested and charged with a crime. He has previously been adjudicated a youthful offender following conviction of a felony.

(DOES NOT QUALIFY. The youth must be less than 19 years old (See "1" in section 720.10).

C. Cecilia Norwin, a female, 17 years old, is arrested and charged with a crime. She had previously been convicted and sentenced for a felony.

(DOES NOT QUALIFY. The section states, "2. Eligible youth means a youth who is eligible to be found a youthful offender. Every youth is so eligible **unless**... (b) such youth has previously been adjudicated a youthful offender following a conviction and sentencing for a felony." Ms. Norwin was previously convicted and sentenced for a felony.)

D. none of the above

(THIS IS THE ANSWER because none of the preceding three persons qualify as a youthful offender.)

Questions 4 - 5

Answer questions 4 - 5 based on the information provided in the following summaries of two Penal Law and Criminal Procedure Law sections.

Penal Law (PL) S 240.40 Appearance in public under the influence of narcotics or a drug other than alcohol.

A person is guilty of appearance in public under the influence of narcotics or a drug other than alcohol when he appears in a public place under the influence of narcotics or a drug other than alcohol to the degree that he may endanger himself or other persons or property, or annoy persons in his vicinity. Appearance in public under the influence of narcotics or a drug other than alcohol is a violation.

Criminal Procedure Law (CPL) S 160.10 When fingerprints may or must be taken

Following an arrest, or following arraignment upon a local criminal court accusatory instrument, a defendant must be fingerprinted where the accusatory instrument charges:

(a) a felony

(b) a misdemeanor defined in the Penal Law

(c) a misdemeanor defined outside of the Penal Law which would constitute a felony if such person had a previous judgment of conviction for a crime

(d) loitering for the purposes of engaging in a prostitution offense (Penal Law 240.37)

After an arrest for any offense, fingerprints may be taken where:

(a) law enforcement is unable to ascertain the person's identity.

(b) identification given by such person may not be accurate.

(c) there is reasonable cause to believe the person might be sought by law enforcement officials for the commission of some other offense.

When fingerprints are required to be taken, photographs and palm prints may be taken.

-----

4. Police Officer Marino arrests a person whom he reasonably believes is appearing in public under the influence of narcotics or a drug other than alcohol and who is annoying persons in his vicinity. The person provides acceptable I.D. (California issued driver's license with photo).

Which of the following choices is correct with respect to requiring fingerprints from the person arrested?

A. Fingerprints must be taken because the person was arrested for an offense.

B. Because fingerprints are required for any arrest as per PL S 240.0, photographs and palm prints may be taken.

C. Fingerprints must be taken because all drug offenses are felonies.

D. CPL S 160.10 does not authorize the taking of fingerprints in this particular instance.

----

5. Police Officer Janet Yaeger arrests a person for loitering for the purposes of engaging in a prostitution offense (Penal Law 240.37). Which of the following four statements is correct?

A. Fingerprints must be taken only if the person is of the age of 18 or over.

B. Fingerprints can only be taken if photographs and palm prints are also taken.

C. Fingerprints must be taken, even if Officer Yaeger personally knows the identity of the person arrested.

D. Photographs and palm prints must be taken.

Answers 4 - 5

4. Police Officer Marino arrests a person whom he reasonably believes is appearing in public under the influence of narcotics or a drug other than alcohol and who is annoying persons in his vicinity. The person provides acceptable I.D. (California issued driver's license with photo).

Which of the following choices is correct with respect to requiring fingerprints from the person arrested?

A. Fingerprints must be taken because the person was arrested for an offense.

(WRONG. Fingerprints must be taken when the arrest is for <u>specified</u> offenses ((a)-(d)) and not for just any offense.)

B. Because fingerprints are required for an arrest as per PL S 240.40, photographs and palm prints may be taken.

(WRONG. PL 240.40 is for a <u>violation</u> (and is not an offense listed in CPL 160.10 ((a)-(d))

C. Fingerprints must be taken because all drug offenses are felonies.

(WRONG. All drug offenses are not felonies. One example is PL S 240, a violation.)

D. CPL S 160.10 does not authorize the taking of fingerprints in this particular instance.

(CORRECT. The offense is a violation, and not an offense specified in CPL 160.10 ((a)-(d)).

----

5. Police Officer Janet Yaeger arrests a person for loitering for the purposes of engaging in a prostitution offense (Penal Law 240.37). Which of the following four statements is correct?

A. Fingerprints must be taken only if the person is of the age of 18 or over.

(WRONG. CPL 160.10 does not specify any minimum age.)

B. Fingerprints can only be taken if photographs and palm prints are also taken.

(WRONG. CPL 160.10 states, "When fingerprints are required to be taken, photographs and palm prints <u>may</u> be taken" – the reverse meaning of answer B.)

C. Fingerprints must be taken, even if Officer Yaeger personally knows the identity of the person arrested.

(CORRECT. CPL 160.10 states "Following an arrest, or following arraignment upon a local criminal court accusatory instrument, a defendant <u>must</u> be fingerprinted where the accusatory instrument charges...<u>loitering for purposes of engaging in a prostitution offense</u>....")

D. Photographs and palm prints must be taken.

(WRONG. CPL 160.10 states, "When fingerprints are required to be taken, photographs and palm prints <u>may</u> be taken.")

CLOZE QUESTIONS 8

The CLOZE section of the test measures your reading ability. It contains passages of text with certain words deleted from the passage. In place of each deleted word, there are a number of dashes (one for each letter of the word that has been deleted).

You are asked to use the "contextual clues" in the paragraph to deduce the missing words.

According to the "Applicant Preparation Guide For the POST Entry-Level Law Enforcement Test Battery" booklet, "A word is considered correct if it is syntactically correct and semantically appropriate...In some instances, there is more than one correct response; in others, only one word can correctly fill the blank." You need to provide only one correct word to get credit for the answer.

Pay careful attention about how to mark your answers on the answer sheet. If you are confused or have any questions, immediately ask the proctor.

CLOZE Test #1 Instructions: In the following passages of text, certain words have been deleted and replaced by dashes (one dash for each letter of the word that has been deleted). Using the "contextual clues" in the paragraph, deduce the missing words and record your answers on the answer sheet, as instructed.

Passage 1:

During 1) _ _ _ month of July 2016 there were nine burglaries reported in Police Officer Callion's patrol area. In two 2) _ _ the burglaries, neighbors reported that at the approximate time of the burglaries they witnessed 3) _ male white, average height, shoulder length, dark hair, "with about a one inch scar 4) _ _ his left cheek." Both times the man was carrying a large brown carton out of the residence that had 5) _ _ _ _ burglarized. They also reported 6) _ _ _ _ at both times he 7) _ _ _ been wearing a blue T-shirt, dark blue, dirty dungarees, 8) _ _ _ white sneakers.

Passage 2:

The ability to remember facts 9) _ _ _ information is important in properly carrying out 10) _ _ _ duties of a Police Officer. All Police 11) _ _ _ _ _ _ _ _ perform security duties and varying amounts of clerical duties, depending 12) _ _ their assignment. 13) _ Police Officer assigned to operating a magnetometer 14) _ _ the main lobby 15) _ _ concerned primarily 16) _ _ _ _ security duties, while a Police Officer assigned 17) _ _ a criminal trial part may be called upon to utilize some clerical skills. 18) _ _ both of these functions, 19) _ _ _ ability to remember a variety 20) _ _ facts and information such as the current case file 21) _ _ _ descriptions of persons, names of attorneys, daily changes in rules and orders, etc., makes it easier for the Police Officer 22) _ _ work effectively.

Passage 3:

After lunch, the trial started with the Judge making opening comments regarding 23) _ _ _ procedures that would 24) _ _ followed, the role of 25) _ _ _ jury, and preliminary remarks regarding the type of case that they would hear. The attorneys then made opening statements. The attorney for the plaintiff spoke for seventeen minutes, followed by Helen

McKenzie, the attorney 26) _ _ _ the defendant, who spoke for fifteen minutes. The first witness called by the plaintiff 27) _ _ _ Winifred Rhodes. She recounted what she saw at 28) _ _ _ intersection of Fulton Street 29) _ _ _ Smith Street, where the auto accident had occurred. The second witness for the plaintiff was Alfred Jones. She also explained 30) _ _ _ _ he had seen. The testimony 31) _ _ Mr. Jones ended at 4:45 P.M., at which time Judge Rodriguez adjourned 32) _ _ _ the day.

Passage 4:

Most police cars 33) _ _ _ modified versions of 34) _ _ _ _ available to 35) _ _ _ general public. Police cars usually are modified cars 36) _ _ _ _ reinforced bumpers, lights, security devices, 37) _ _ _ other equipment, including radios and suspect separator bars and shields. Some police cars receive special modification. These cars include those 38) _ _ _ _ transport police dogs or bomb squads. Because 39) _ _ the heavy use of police cars, 40) _ _ _ _ _ service lifetime 41) _ _ shorter than that of cars used 42) _ _ the general public. However, 43) _ _ _ shortened service time 44) _ _ _ the extra cost of the modifications are more than made up by increased safety 45) _ _ _ greater police effectiveness.

Answer for Questions 1-45:

1. the	16. with	31.of
2. of	17. to	32. for
3. a	18. In	33. are
4. on	19. the	34. cars
5. been	20. of	35. the
6. that	21. and	36. with
7. had	22. to	37. and
8. and	23. the	38. that
9. and	24. be	39. of
10. the	25. the	40. their
11. Officers	26. for	41. is
12. on	27. was	42. by
13. A	28. the	43. the
14. in	29. and	44. and
15. is	30. what	45. and

CALIFORNIA POST EXAM GUIDE (PELLETB)

CLOZE Test #2 Instructions: In the following passages of text, certain words have been deleted and replaced by dashes (one dash for each letter of the word that has been deleted). Using the "contextual clues" in the paragraph, deduce the missing words and record your answers on the answer sheet, as instructed.

Passage 1:

A prosecution 1) _ _ _ any felony must 2) _ _ commenced within 5 years of commission of 3) _ _ _ offense. Where the offense is 4) _ misdemeanor, for the commencement of a criminal action to be timely, 5) _ _ accusatory instrument must be filed within 2 years following the commission 6) _ _ the offense. Where the offense charged is aggravated sexual abuse in first degree (130.70 PL), for the commencement of a criminal action to 7) _ _ timely, an accusatory 8) _ _ _ _ _ _ _ _ _ _ may be filed at any time following the commission of the offense. Where the offense is a petty offense, for 9) _ _ _ commencement of a criminal action to 10) _ _ timely, 11) _ _ accusatory instrument must be filed within one year following 12) _ _ _ commission of the offense.

Passage 2:

Arraignment 13) _ _ the process by which a criminal court acquires personal jurisdiction over a defendant (a person charged 14) _ _ _ _ having committed a criminal offense). A person arrested 15) _ _ _ allegedly committing a felony is first arraigned in one of 16) _ _ _ lower criminal courts. If the case is not disposed of at arraignment, 17) _ _ _ person's future attendance is secured 18) _ _ _ the case is transferred 19) _ _ the grand jury. A 20) _ _ _ _ _ _ jury is a body of 16 21) _ _ 23 citizens who review the charges 22) _ _ _ decide whether 23) _ _ not to order the filing of 24) _ _ indictment. The filing of an indictment 25) _ _ a requirement for the prosecution of 26) _ _ _ felony in one 27) _ _ the superior criminal courts.

Passage 3:

28) _ _ _ possibility of promotion 29) _ _ a major incentive to enter the police force. Because of retirements and other reasons, frequent promotional opportunities become available. In civil service, many promotions require success on a 30) _ _ _ _ _ service exam, as well 31) _ _ meeting other standards. 32) _ _ _ example, in some jurisdictions police officers must complete two or more years as a patrolman 33) _ _ qualify to sit for the sergeant

74

exam. In many jurisdictions, higher police officer titles such 34) _ _ Captain, Major, 35) _ _ _ above require the analysis of 36) _ _ _ candidate's career achievements and the endorsement of job interview panels.

Passage 4:

Many municipalities 37) _ _ _ counties offer police officers excellent retirement plans. Although historically a large percentage 38) _ _ officers took advantage of early retirement plans, 39) _ _ _ trend in the past few decades has been for officers to postpone their retirement 40) _ _ _ _ the force. One of the major reasons is that the average life expectancy has increased 41) _ _ _ officers 42) _ _ _ reluctant 43) _ _ secure their later years primarily 44) _ _ _ _ the civil service pension. Also, with increasing medical advances, 45) _ _ _ "I still feel good" perception of older officers has been increasing.

Answer for Questions 1-45:

1. for	16. the	31. as
2. be	17. the	32. for
3. the	18. and	33. to
4. a	19. to	34. as
5. an	20. grand	35. and
6. of	21. to	36. the
7. be	22. and	37. and
8. instrument	23. or	38. of
9. the	24. an	39. the
10. be	25. is	40. from
11. an	26. the, any	41. and
12. the	27. of	42. are
13. is	28. the	43. to
14. with	29. is	44. with
15. for	30. civil	45. the

CALIFORNIA POST EXAM GUIDE (PELLETB)

CLOZE Test #3 Instructions: In the following passages of text, certain words have been deleted and replaced by dashes (one dash for each letter of the word that has been deleted). Using the "contextual clues" in the paragraph, deduce the missing words and record your answers on the answer sheet, as instructed.

Passage 1:

Job seekers often make 1) _ _ _ mistake not considering a civil service job. Many individuals who 2) _ _ _ presently unemployed want to secure a job 3) _ _ soon as possible and are not 4) _ _ a frame 5) _ _ mind to study for a 6) _ _ _ _ _ service position, and take the test, and then wait to be considered 7) _ _ _ a position. However, in 8) _ _ _ current economic environment with a shortage of quality jobs, it 9) _ _ highly advisable 10) _ _ _ _ such individuals consider civil service.

Passage 2:

Applying 11) _ _ _ a civil service job that is awarded 12) _ _ successful exam candidates who meet all job requirements 13) _ _ advisable for a number 14) _ _ reasons. Although civil 15) _ _ _ _ _ _ _ positions 16) _ _ _ obtained after a lengthy screening process, 17) _ _ _ waiting is well worth it. Besides the increased 18) _ _ _ security (as compared to jobs in 19) _ _ _ private sector), civil service 20) _ _ _ _ often come 21) _ _ _ _ significant benefits. One of the most important of these 22) _ _ _ _ _ _ _ _ is a generous pension.

Passage 3:

Civil service pensions are usually contributory. That is, employees contribute 23) _ certain percentage of their income. That 24) _ _ _ _ _ _ _ _ _ _ is usually supplemented 25) _ _ contributions of the government employer. It 26) _ _ not unusual to see employees retire after 20 or 30 years with generous pensions. This is especially true for peace officers and police officers 27) _ _ _ usually qualify for a pension after only 20 years of service.

Passage 4:

In addition, 28) _ _ a generous pension, employees 29) _ _ _ eligible for quality medical 30) _ _ _ dental insurance. Paid vacation days and paid sick days add to 31) _ _ _ desirability of civil service 32) _ _ _ _ _. For all 33) _ _ _ above reasons, it is not unusual to see more than

34) _ _ _ generation of a family working 35) _ _ civil service. This 36) _ _ especially true 37) _ _ _ certain professions such 38) _ _ police officers 39) _ _ _ teachers.

Passage 5:

Anyone interested 40) _ _ obtaining a civil service 41) _ _ _ can find information on employment web sites hosted 42) _ _ local, state, and federal agencies. All the sites contain information 43) _ _ the variety 44) _ _ jobs offered and how to apply 45) _ _ _ them.

Answer for Questions 1-45:

1. the	16. are	31. the
2. are	17. the	32. jobs
3. as	18. job	33. the
4. in	19. the	34. one
5. of	20. jobs	35. in
6. civil	21. with	36. is
7. for	22. benefits	37. for
8. the	23. a	38. as
9. is	24. percentage	39. and
10. that	25. by	40. in
11. for	26. is	41. job
12. to	27. who	42. by
13. is	28. to	43. on
14. of	29. are	44. of
15.service	30.and	45. for

REASONING

9

The following types of questions are included in "Reasoning Questions":

1. Deductive and Inductive Reasoning

2. Number series (number patterns)

3. Comparisons and differences of words, and

4. Seeing the hierarchy or order of objects, rules, events, etc.

1. Deductive and Inductive Reasoning

Deductive Reasoning questions evaluate a candidate's ability to understand general rules and apply them to specific situations.

Inductive Reasoning questions evaluate a candidate's ability to combine details or separate pieces of information to form general rules.

Because both of these types of questions rely heavily on reading comprehension, they are included in the passages in Section 7 (Reading Comprehension).

In this section we will discuss the three remaining types of "Reasoning Questions."

• Number series patterns

• Comparisons and Differences of words and Concepts (Example of question: Which of the following four does not fit with the other three?)

• Hierarchy of objects, rules, etc. (Ascending, descending order, place within the group, etc.)

———————

Number Series

Number series questions require you to:

1. concentrate on a series of numbers,

2. see what relationship (pattern) exists among the numbers,

3. determine what are the next numbers in the series.

Although advanced math is not required, a knowledge of simple arithmetic (addition, subtraction, multiplication, and division) will increase your speed and accuracy and thereby increase your score.

Questions to ask yourself when you are considering a number series: What is the difference between the numbers in the series? Are the numbers increasing or decreasing? If so, are they increasing or decreasing by the same amount - or a different amount that is perhaps itself increasing or decreasing? Are there two or more alternating series?

The key to doing well in this type of question is in SEEING THE PATTERN.

The following examples will help you to see the patterns:

The pattern can be simple or complicated. An example of the simplest pattern is the following:

A) 7   7   7   7   7   __

The pattern in number series A) is the number 7 REPEATED.

The next number in the number series is 7.

What are the next two numbers in number series B?

B)   4   4   4   4   4   __ __

The pattern is the number 4 REPEATED.

The next two numbers in this number series are 4 and 4. Simple enough.

Now let us go one step further: Two alternating simple patterns. For example:

    C)   7 4 7 4 7 4 __ __

The pattern is the number 7 and 4 ALTERNATING.

The next two numbers in this number series are 7 and 4.

Here is a more complex version of number series C).

    D)   7 7 4 4 7 7 4 4 __ __

The pattern here are the two DOUBLE numbers of 7 and 4 (77 and 44) ALTERNATING.

The next two numbers in this number series are 7 and 7.

Now, let's take the above number series A), B), C) and D) and go one step further.

    A)   7 8 9 10 11 12 __ __

The pattern is 7 INCREASING by 1 each time. The 2 final numbers are 13 and 14.

    B)   4 5 6 7 8 __ __

    The pattern is 4 INCREASING by 1 each time. The next 2 numbers in this number series are 9 and 10.

    C)   7 4 8 5 9 6 __ __

The pattern is 7 and 4 ALTERNATING AND INCREASING BY 1 each time.

The next 2 numbers are 10 and 7.

Now, let's take number series A), B), C) and D) and ask more difficult questions:

    A)   7 6 5 4 3 2 __ __

The pattern is 7 DECREASING by 1 each time.

The next 2 numbers in this number series are 1 and 0.

B)   5   4   3   2   __ __

The pattern is 5 DECREASING by 1 each time.

The next 2 numbers in this number series are 1 and 0.

C)   7   4   6   3   5   2   __ __

The pattern is 7 and 4 ALTERNATING AND DECREASING BY 1 each time

The next 2 numbers in this number series are 4 and 1.

• **Keep in mind that in a pattern, numbers can be added, subtracted, divided, or multiplied and that in some examples there can be an alternating pattern.**

• **Please note also that some of the following number patterns have been designed to be more difficult than the average difficulty level of number patterns.**

The following are 5 Number Series questions which you are to answer. For each number series, you are to figure out the pattern in the series so that you will be able to determine what two numbers would be the last two numbers in the series.

1)   80 50 75 45 71 41   __ _

A) 68, 37   B) 69, 36   C) 68, 38   D) 68, 36   E) 69, 37

2)   60 64 68 72 76 80   __ __

A) 82, 86   B) 83, 87   C) 84, 86   D) 84, 88   E) 83, 86

3)   1 3 9 27   __ __

A) 81, 242   B) 80, 243   C) 79, 247   D) 81, 244   E) 81, 243

4)   30 30 34 34 38 38 42 42   __ __

A) 46, 46   B) 47, 47   C) 48, 48   D) 46, 47   E) 47, 46

5)   93 84 76 69 63 58 __ __

A) 53, 51   B) 54, 51   C) 54, 52   D) 52, 53   E) 52, 51

Answers 1-5

1. C (68, 38)

Pattern is two DOUBLE numbers (80 and 50) ALTERNATING and DECREASING by a DECREASING amount (first decreasing by 5, then decreasing by 4, then decreasing by 3....).

2. D (84, 88)

Pattern is the number 60 INCREASING by 4 each time the pattern is repeated.

3. E (81, 243)

Pattern is 1 MULTIPLIED by 3 each time the pattern is repeated (1 X 3 = 3, 3 X 3 = 9, 9 X 3 = 27, 27 X 3 = 81, 81 X 3 = 243).

4. A (46, 46)

The pattern is the number 30 REPEATED once and then INCREASED by 4 each time the pattern is repeated (30, Repeat 30, 30 + 4 = 34, Repeat 34, 34 + 4 = 38, Repeat 38, 38 + 4 = 42, Repeat 42, 42 + 4 = 46, Repeat 46).

5. B (54, 51)

The pattern is the number 93 DECREASING by a DECREASING number each time the pattern is repeated (93 - 9 = 84, 84 - 8 = 76, 76 - 7 = 69, 69 - 6 = 63, 63 - 5 = 58, 58 - 4 = 54, 54 - 3 = 51).

Comparisons and Differences of Words and Concepts

Directions: For the following question, select the choice containing the word that does not belong in the group of the other three words.

Example:

A. taste

B. smell

C. touch

D. ear (The other 3 words are senses. Ear is a body part.)

Answer: D. ear (Taste, smell, and touch refer to the senses. Ear is a part of the body.)

Questions 1-5

Directions: For the following five questions, select the choice containing the word that does not belong in the group of the other three words.

Question 1:

A. taste

B. smell

C. feel

D. ear

Question 2:

A. social club

B. restaurant

C. bar

D. table

Question 3:

A. shoes

B. slippers

C. pants

D. moccasins

Question 4:

A. Sergeant

B. Captain

C. Corporal

D. Medal

Question 5:

A. juvenile

B. youth

C. kid

D. elder

Answers 1-5

Directions: For the following five questions, select the choice containing the word that does not belong in the group of the other three words.

Answer 1:

A. taste

B. smell

C. feel

D. ear (The other 3 words are senses. Ear is a body part.)

Answer 2:

A. social club

B. restaurant

C. bar

D. table (The other 3 words are places, generally where people meet. Table is an object that can be found anywhere.)

Answer 3:

A. shoes

B. slippers

C. pants (The other 3 words are items worn on the feet. Pants are for the legs.)

D. moccasins

Answer 4:

A. Sergeant

B. Captain

C. Corporal

D. Medal (The other 3 words are military titles. Medal is an object awarded for merit.)

Answer 5:

A. juvenile

B. youth

C. kid

D. elder (The other 3 words relate to young people. Elder refers to someone who is old.)

Questions 6-10

Directions: For the following five questions, select the choice containing the word that does not belong in the group of the other three words.

Question 6:

A. felony

B. misdemeanor

C. infraction

D. criminal

Question 7:

A. accomplice

B. student

C. lookout

D. collaborator

Question 8:

A. store

B. eater

C. shop

D. mall

Question 9:

A. sister

B. salesman

C. cousin

D. nephew

Question 10:

A. upward

B. right

C. car

D. left

Answers 6-10

Directions: For the following five questions, select the choice containing the word that does not belong in the group of the other three words.

Answer 6:

A. felony

B. misdemeanor

C. infraction

D. criminal (The other 3 words are types of offenses. Criminal refers to a person.)

Answer 7:

A. accomplice

B. student (The other 3 words relate to criminal associates. This word describes a person who is learning.)

C. lookout

D. collaborator

Answer 8:

A. store

B. eater (The other 3 words refer to places where one can buy things. Eater refers to someone who feeds.)

C. shop

D. mall

Answer 9:

A. sister

B. salesman (The other 3 words refer to relatives. Salesman is an occupation.)

C. cousin

D. nephew

Answer 10:

A. upward

B. right

C. car (The other 3 words are spatial directions. Car is an object.)

D. left

_____

Understanding the Order of Things

Information Ordering

These questions evaluate your ability to put in order given rules or actions. The rules or actions can include letters, words, sentences, procedures, pictures, and logical or mathematical operations.

The key to answering this type of question correctly is to make sure that the directions are clear to you.

To obtain maximum clarity, take the time to understand the logical order of the directions. Steps that must be done "before" or "after" or "at the same time" should be noted.

Also, at the time of selecting your answer, refer to the directions to make sure that you have not mentally mixed up the order or the details of the directions.

Question 1

Four face masks used in burglaries were discovered at the suspect's house. One was black. One was dark grey. One was light grey. One was white. Which color mask is the third darkest?

A. black

B. dark grey

C. white

D. light grey

Answer 1

B. dark grey

(The order of darkness of the masks is: white (1), light grey (2), dark grey (3), black (4).)

Question 2

Answer question 2 based on the following "Bomb Threat Procedure."

Bomb Threat Procedure

Some bomb threats are received by phone. A Police Officer who receives a bomb threat by phone should do the following in the order specified:

1. Stay calm. Do not hang up, even if the caller hangs up. Be polite and show interest in what the caller is saying.

2. If possible, write a message to a fellow officer or other Police Department employee.

3. If your phone displays the caller number, write down the number.

4. Even if the caller hangs up, do not hang up your phone. Use a different phone that is not a cell phone to contact the "Bomb Threat Notification Unit."

-----

2. At a "Bomb Threat Exercise", you are told that you have answered a phone call during which a bomb threat is made. You have written a note and notified a Police Officer working at the desk next to yours. You have also written down the caller's number which displayed on your phone unit. The caller hangs up. The next step you should take is to:

A. Hang up the phone and immediately call the "Bomb Threat Notification Unit."

B. Do not hang up the phone, but use a cell phone to contact the "Bomb Threat Notification Unit."

C. Complete the form "Bomb Threat Checklist."

D. Do not hang up and use a different phone (not a cell phone) to contact the "Bomb Threat Notification Unit."

Answer 2

1. At a "Bomb Threat Exercise," you are told that you have answered a phone call during which a bomb threat is made. You have written a note and notified a Police Officer working at the desk next to yours. You have also written down the caller's number which displayed on your phone unit. The caller hangs up. The next step you should take is to:

A. Hang up the phone and immediately call the "Bomb Threat Notification Unit."

(WRONG. Number 1 states, "Do <u>not</u> hang up...")

B. Do not hang up the phone, but use a cell phone to contact the "Bomb Threat Notification Unit."

(WRONG. Number 3 states, "Use a different phone that is <u>not</u> a cell phone...")

C. Complete the form "Bomb Threat Checklist."

(WRONG. Number 5 states, "complete the form "Bomb Threat Checklist." This is the <u>last</u> step and is done <u>after</u> contacting the "Bomb Threat Notification Unit.")

<u>D. Do not hang up and use a different phone (not a cell phone) to contact the "Bomb Threat Notification Unit."</u>

(**CORRECT.** This is step number four and comes directly after step number three, "...write down the number," which you have already done.)

Question 3

Your sergeant gives you five "Complaint Forms" with the following priority numbers:

2867   19643   0344   783   8249

He asks you to organize the forms in ascending priority.

According to the above, the third Complaint Form would be Complaint Form number:

A. 8249   C. 783

B. 2867   D. 0344

Answer 3

Examples of ascending order and descending order

Ascending Priority Number Order	Descending Priority Number Order
1	5
2	4
3	3
4	2
5	1

The Complaint Forms in Ascending Priority Number Order are as follows:

1) 0344

2) 783

3) 2867

4) 8249

5) 19643

The third complaint number on the list is 2867, therefore the correct answer is **B) 2867**.

Question 4

Your sergeant gives you five "Requests for Investigation" forms submitted by residents in your precinct. The forms were submitted by the following five persons:

George Felder, Harriet Volker, Ben Halston, Abe Johnson, Diane Molton

He asks you to organize the forms in last name alphabetical order.

According to the above, the fourth "Request for Investigation" form is the one submitted by:

A. Halston, Ben

B. Volker, Harriet

C. Molton, Diane

D. Felder, George

Answer 4

The correct listing in last name alphabetical order is:

1) Felder, George
2) Halston, Ben
3) Johnson, Abe
4) Molton, Diane
5) Volker, Harriet

The fourth name on the list is Molton, Diane, therefore the correct answer is **C) Molton, Diane**.

Question 5

5. The ninth letter of the alphabet is:

A) H

B) J

C) I

D. G

Answer 5

The letters of the alphabet (in order) are as follows:

A,   B,   C,   D,   E,   F,   G,   H,   I   J,   K,   L   M.....
1........2........3........4......5........6.........7........8........**9**.......10.......11.......12.......13....
The correct answer is **C) I.**

Question 6

You are assigned to drive the precinct van. Your sergeant asks you to make five stops to pick up police officers. At the first two stops you are to pick up six police officers at each stop. At the last three stops you are to pick up four police officers at each stop. Which of the following mathematical expressions correctly states the total number of police officers that you will pick up at the five stops?

A) 2 + 6 + 3 + 4   B) 2 X 6 X 3 X 4   C) 2 + 3   D) 2(6) + 3(4)

Answer 6

At the first two stops you will pick up six police officers at each stop (6 + 6 = 12 police officers). At the last three stops you will pick up 4 police officers at each stop (4 + 4 + 4 = 12 police officers). The total number of police officers to be picked up is therefore 24 (because 12 + 12 = 24 police officers).

The A, B, C, and D choices would yield the following results:

A) 2 + 6 + 3 + 4 (This gives a total of 15).

B) 2 X 6 X 3 X 4 (This gives a total of 144.)

C) 2 + 3 (This gives a total of 5.)

D) 2(6) + 3(4) = 24

(The mathematical expression 2(6) + 3(4) means (2 X 6) + (3 X 4) = 24. The correct answer therefore is **D) 2(6) + 3(4)**.)

Question 7

Organize the following four sentences in the best logical order:

1. This training includes classroom and "on the street" practice driving.

2. Because of this, they receive proper driving and safety instruction.

3. "On the street" driving is stressed and comprises eighty percent of the training time.

4. Police Officers may be assigned to drive a precinct van.

(A) 1, 3, 4, 2   (B) 2, 3, 4, 1   (C) 3, 2, 1, 4   (D) 4, 2, 1, 3

Answer 7

The correct answer is **(D) 4, 2, 1, 3.**

4. Police Officers may be assigned to drive a precinct van. (This sentence introduces the topic of driving a precinct van.)

2. Because of this, they receive proper driving and safety instruction.

1. This training includes classroom and "on the street" practice driving.

3. "On the street" driving is stressed and comprises eighty percent of the training time.

(After sentence 4, sentences 2, 1, and 3 follow logically in that order.)

Question 8

Your sergeant hands you five "Overtime Request Forms" which you submitted for processing. He reminds you that all overtime requests must be submitted in date order and numbered sequentially. The dates on the overtime forms are as follows:

10-4-2016   9/24/2016   October 1, 2016   September 28, 2016   Sept. 12, 2016

He asks you to number the forms in ascending date order and that you resubmit them. Assume that you organize the forms as your supervisor asks and that you also number the first request "Request 1," which of the above dated requests would be numbered "Request 3"?

A. 10-4-2016

B. 9/24/2016

C. October 1, 20146

D. September 28, 2016

Answer 8

The correct ascending date order is:

1) Sept. 12, 2016

2) 9/24/2016

3) September 28, 2016

4) October 1, 2016

5) 10-4-2016

The third date on the list is September 28, 2016. Therefore, the correct answer is

D). September 28, 2016.

Question 9

The following are four sentences. Each sentence (listed in random order) is one of the four steps necessary to attach a metal shield to the front of a van. Which one of the following choices (A, B, C, D) lists the order of sentences which best expresses the logical sequence of metal shield installation?

4 1. Drive the van slowly forward to test whether the shield is securely bolted to the van.

3 2. Tighten the bolts with heavy duty nuts.

1 3. Align the front of the van with the shield connectors.

2 4. Insert connecting bolts in aligned holes of shield and the van's shield connectors.

A. 1, 4, 2, 3

B. 2, 3, 4, 1

C. 4, 1, 3, 2

D. 3, 4, 2, 1

Answer 9

The correct answer is **D. 3, 4, 2, 1.** (In this order, the sentences are logically connected.)

3. Align the front of the van with the shield connectors.

4. Insert connecting bolts in aligned holes of shield and the van's shield connector.

2. Tighten the bolts with heavy duty nuts.

1. Drive the van slowly forward to test whether the shield is securely bolted to the van.

———————

IMPORTANT WORDS | 10

Try to become familiar with the following list. It contains important <u>spelling</u> and <u>vocabulary</u> words for police officers. Try to study this list during brief study sessions (as opposed to a few long study sessions.) There is a theory of learning which states that students remember most when they study for short periods instead of one long period. Therefore, seven study periods during the week are more effective than one long period during the weekend.

• abide	• aggression	• atheist
• absence	• aggressive	• assassination
• acceptable	• alias	• assailant
• accessory	• alibi	• assassination
• accident	• allegation	• atheist
• accidentally	• alleged	• August
• accommodate	• allegiance	• autopsy
• accomplice	• almost	• awful
• achieve	• amateur	• battery
• acknowledge	• ambulance	• because
• acquaintance	• analysis	• becoming
• acquainted	• angle	• beginning
• acquire	• annotate	• believe
• acquit	• annually	• belligerent
• acreage	• apparent	• bellwether
• address	• apparently	• benevolent
• adjacent	• apprised	• bicycle
• admonish	• approach	• boisterous
• adultery	• arctic	• burglary
• adversary	• argument	• business
• advisable	• arraign	• calendar
• affect	• arrest	• caliber
• affidavit	• arson	• camouflage
• aggravated	• asphalt	• capitol

CALIFORNIA POST EXAM GUIDE (PELLETB)

- Caribbean
- category
- Caucasian
- caught
- cemetery
- changeable
- chief
- coerce
- colleague
- collectible
- collision
- column
- coming
- commit
- committed
- concealed
- concede
- congratulate
- conscientious
- conscious
- consensus
- consideration
- contempt
- continuing
- controlling
- controversy
- contusion
- conviction
- coolly
- coroner
- corroborate
- countenance
- counterfeit
- credulity

- culprit
- cumbersome
- curfew
- deceive
- defamation
- definitely
- delinquent
- derision
- desist
- desperate
- detain
- deterrent
- difference
- dilapidated
- dilemma
- disappear
- disappoint
- disastrous
- discernable
- disheveled
- disorderly
- disperse
- disturbance
- drown
- drunkenness
- dumbbell
- embarrass
- embezzlement
- emulate
- enamored
- enigma
- epilepsy
- equipment
- erratic

- exceed
- exhaust
- exhibit
- exhilarate
- existence
- exonerate
- experience
- extort
- extradition
- extreme
- famished
- farthest
- fascinating
- February
- felonious
- fictitious
- fiery
- flippant
- fluorescent
- fondle
- forcible
- foreign
- forgery
- formidable
- friend
- fugitive
- fulfil
- gauge
- government
- grateful
- guarantee
- guidance
- handicapped
- harass

- harassed
- height
- heroin
- hierarchy
- hindrance
- homicide
- humorous
- hygiene
- hypodermic
- hysterical
- ignorance
- illicit
- illiterate
- imaginary
- imbued
- imitate
- immediately
- impetuous
- incessant
- incidentally
- incoherent
- incriminating
- incursion
- independent
- indictment
- indispensable
- informant
- inhabited
- innocence
- inoculate
- insidious
- intelligence
- interfering
- interrogation

- intruder
- irrational
- jewelry
- judgment
- jurisdiction
- kernel
- laboratory
- laceration
- leisure
- lethal
- lethargic
- liaison
- library
- license
- lightning
- lose
- maintain
- maintenance
- malicious
- manslaughter
- memento
- militant
- millennium
- miniature
- minuscule
- miscellaneous
- mischief
- mischievous
- misdemeanor
- misspell
- necessary
- negligent
- neighbor
- niece

- noticeable
- notify
- obscene
- obstruct
- obvious
- occasion
- occasionally
- occurred
- occurrence
- occult
- offender
- omission
- opinion
- opium
- original
- outrageous
- pallid
- pamphlet
- paralyze
- parliament
- pastime
- perceive
- perjury
- perpetrator
- perseverance
- persistent
- personnel
- plagiarize
- playwright
- plead
- possession
- potatoes
- precede
- precedent

- prescription
- presence
- prevalent
- principle
- privilege
- probable cause
- prodigious
- professor
- prolific
- promise
- pronunciation
- proof
- prosecute
- protruding
- publicly
- puncture
- pursuit
- quarantine
- quarrel
- questionnaire
- readable
- really
- receipt
- receive
- recollection
- recommend
- reconciliation
- recurrence
- refer
- reference
- referred
- refrigerator
- registration

- regress
- relevant
- religious
- rendezvous
- repetition
- repudiate
- respiration
- restaurant
- restitution
- resuscitation
- rhyme
- rhythm
- ridiculous
- scarcely
- schedule
- secretary
- seize
- seizure
- separate
- sergeant
- siege
- significance
- silhouette
- similar
- simultaneous
- sparse
- specimen
- speech
- straighten
- strength
- subpoena
- subsidiary
- successful

- suicide
- summons
- superstitious
- suppress
- surprise
- surprised
- surveillance
- suspicious
- swerve
- syringe
- tattoo
- testify
- tetanus
- thieve
- thirtieth
- thorough
- Thursday
- tomatoes
- tomorrow
- transient
- traumatic
- Tuesday
- turbulent
- turmoil
- twelfth
- tyranny
- unconscious
- underrate
- unequivocal
- unforeseen
- until
- upholstery

- vacuum • vandalize • vehicle • vehicular • vicinity • vicious • visible • warrant • weather • Wednesday • weird • welfare • whether • withhold

PRACTICE TEST #1 QUESTIONS   11

Instructions: For questions 1–15, select the choice with the correct spelling of the omitted word in the preceding sentence.

1.The officer told the teenager that his behavior was not _____.

A. aceptible

B. acceptable

C. acceptabel

D. acceptibel

-----

2. Marking appointments on the _____ is a good way to be reminded of them.

A. callander

B. calender

C. callender

D. calendar

-----

3. Based on the evidence, the jury did not _____ that he was guilty.

A. believe

B. beleve

C. belive

D. beleive

-----

4. He scheduled his vacation during the month of _____.

A. Agoust

B. Augost

C. Augest

D. August

CALIFORNIA POST EXAM GUIDE (PELLETB)

5. They arrived and found him _____.

A. unconscious

B. unconcious

C. unconscius

D. unconcious

-----

6. She was _____ by him because he looked like an honest person.

A. decieved

B. deceived

C. dicieved

D. diceived

---

7. They concluded that he _____ committed the act.

A. definately

B. definitly

C. deffinately

D. definitely

-----

8. His confession placed her in a _____.

A. dilema

B. dilemma

C. delema

D. dealemma

-----

9. The cracks in the door frame indicated _____ entry.

A. forcibele

B. forcible

C. forceable

D. forcable

-----

10. The coroner found a _____ object in her shoulder blade.

A. foreign

B. forriegn

C. forreign

D. foriegn

-----

11. There is no _____ that the search will yield any results.

A. garantee

B. garanty

C. garentee

D. guarantee

-----

12. CIA _____ has found that he is a menber of a terrorist cell.

A. intelegence

B. intelligence

C. intligence

D. intellegence

-----

13. The two robbers are holding three hostages in back of the _____ store

A. juelry

B. jewelry

C. jewellery

D. jewelery

-----

14. The _____ child broke the window by mistake.

A. mischeivous

B. mischevous

C. mischevious

D. mischievous

-----

15. He apologized for the _____ in his report.

A. ommission

B. omision

C. omission

D. ommision

Instructions: For questions 16-30, choose the word that is closest in meaning to the underlined word in the sentence.

16. The sergeant asked the crowd to disperse.

A. gather

B. assemble

C. congregate

D. scatter

-----

17. The novice criminal wanted to emulate his senior partner.

A. condemn

B. jostle

C. imitate

D. deride

-----

18. Because of the medication, his motions were erratic.

A. irregular

B. predictable

C. ordinary

D. consistent

-----

19. He said he stole the bags of cookies because he was famished.

A. stuffed

B. starving

C. satiated

D. satisfied

-----

20. He was guilty of conducting an illicit affair.

A. legal

B. proper

C. legitimate

D. illegal

-----

21. His actions were <u>incriminating</u>.

A. absolving

B. exonerating

C. damning

D. clearing

-----

22. The <u>incursion</u> of the gang into the other gang's territory was the reason for the gang war.

A. intrusion

B. departure

C. exit

D. egress

-----

23. His constant lying eliminated the possibility of any <u>credulity</u>.

A. trust

B. disbelief

C. suspicion

D. mistrust

-----

24. The house was small and <u>dilapidated</u>.

A. undamaged

B. shabby

C. mended

D. intact

-----

25. The license plate was so far away that the numbers were not <u>discernable</u>.

A. unclear

B. invisible

C. distinguishable

D. unperceivable

-----

26. The statements that he made were all <u>fictitious</u>.

A. real

B. true

C. genuine

D. unreal

-----

27. After examining the door, it was clear that the entry had been <u>forcible</u>.

A. violent

B. forceless

C. weak

D. delicate

-----

28. Only one of the rooms was <u>inhabited</u>.

A. deserted

B. abandoned

C. forsaken

D. occupied

-----

29. It was a <u>malicious</u> attempt to destroy her credibility.

A. kind

B. benevolent

C. wicked

D. benign

-----

30. The <u>prescription</u> vial lay on the table.

A. drug

B. poison

C. liquid

D. premium

Instructions: For the following questions 15 questions, (Questions 31-45), decide which sentence is most clearly written.

Choose "A" if sentence "a" is clearer than sentence "b".
Choose "B" if sentence "b" is clearer than sentence "a".

Question 31:

a. Spotting the gunman behind the crates, his heart beat faster.

b. When he spotted the gunman behind the crates, the officer's heart beat faster.

Question 32:

a. Even the officers who were tired took turns at guard duty.

b. The officers took turns at guard duty. Even the officers that were tired.

Question 33:

a. The bank manager thanked the officer for searching for his missing gun.

b. The bank manager thanked the officer for searching for the bank manager's missing gun.

Question 34:

a. Feeling very frightened, the throat dried up.

b. Because the officer was feeling frightened, the officer's throat dried up.

Question 35:

a. Aided by the four teenagers, the officer was able to carry the chest.

b. The officer was able to carry the chest. Aided by the four teenagers.

Question 36:

a. The demonstrators marched in the street, the police officers walked on the sidewalk.

b. The demonstrators marched in the street. The police officers walked on the sidewalk.

Question 37:

a. Trying to avoid the rocks, the truck offered a good shield.

b. Trying to avoid the rocks, the officer used the truck as a shield.

Question 38:

a. The witness liked the attorney as did the D.A.

b. The witness liked the attorney as much as the D.A.

Question 39:

a. After the officer and the rioter fought, the officer's finger started bleeding.

b. After the officer fought with the rioter, his finger started bleeding.

Question 40:

a. The squad radio was malfunctioning every day. It needed to be repaired.

b. The squad radio was malfunctioning every day, it needed to be repaired.

Question 41:

a. Blowing out black fumes, Officer Carlton turned off the emergency switch.

b. Because the furnace was blowing out black fumes, Officer Carlton turned off the emergency switch.

Question 42:

a. The work shift was long and tiresome, especially the last two hours.

b. The work shift was long and tiresome. Especially the last two hours.

Question 43:

a. Because his uniform was stained by the red rioter's paint, he had it dry cleaned.

b. Because his uniform was stained by the rioter's red paint, he had it dry cleaned.

Question 44:

a. He ate cookies and drank soda. Waiting for his mother to pick him up.

b. While waiting for his mother to pick him up, he ate cookies and drank soda.

Question 45:

a. After placing the evidence in the envelope, he took it to his squad car.

b. After placing the evidence in the envelope, he took the envelope to his squad car.

For questions 46-47, read the following passage and then answer the questions based solely on the information provided in the passage.

There is a county court in each county outside the capital city. The county court has limited jurisdiction in civil cases. It may try cases where the amount sued for does not exceed $25,000.00. The county court is also authorized to handle the prosecution of crimes that have been committed inside the county. To lessen the administrative burden posed by the arraignment and preliminary proceedings in numerous criminal cases, courts of limited jurisdiction lower than that of the county court usually handle these initial steps in the criminal prosecution process.

-----

46. Which of the following statements is supported by the above paragraph?

A. The county court in a capital city has a maximum jurisdiction of $25,000.00.

B. County Courts do not handle the initial steps in the criminal prosecution process.

C. Arraignments are handled by the San Francisco Supreme Court.

D. County courts handle both civil and criminal cases within their jurisdiction.

----

47. Which of the following statements is not correct?

A. The capital city does not have a county court.

B. The county court is authorized to handle the prosecution of crimes committed outside the county.

C. The county court can handle some civil cases.

D. The county court can try cases where the amount sued for is $10,000.

For questions 48-49, read the following passage and then answer the questions based solely on the information provided in the passage.

Felonies are the highest type of crimes. The other category of crimes, misdemeanors, are crimes which expose the perpetrator to jail terms which are less than those imposed for felonies. For example, the highest term of imprisonment that can be imposed for a misdemeanor conviction is one year. Felonies can subject the perpetrator to imprisonment of up to life imprisonment or even death.

-----

48. Which of the following statements is supported by the above passage?

A. Jostling in the first degree is a felony.

B. "A" misdemeanors are more severe than "B" misdemeanors.

C. Misdemeanors are crimes of greater severity than petty offenses.

D. Misdemeanors and felonies are crimes.

----

49. Which of the following statements is not correct?

A. Felonies are crimes.

B. A misdemeanor prison sentence may be for a one year term.

C. Imprisonment for a felony must be for less than a year.

D. A sentence for a felony may be death.

For questions 50-51, read the following passage and then answer the questions based solely on the information provided in the passage.

Family Court handles different types of proceedings. One of the most numerous type of proceeding is juvenile delinquency proceedings. A juvenile delinquent is defined as a person over the age of 7 and less than 15 who commits an act which would be a crime if the person were over the age of 15. After a fact-finding hearing, if the court finds that the person committed the act, and if it also finds that the person needs supervision, treatment or confinement, then the court must find that the person is a juvenile delinquent and must make an order prescribing the required supervision, treatment or confinement.

-----

50. Which of the following statements is not correct as per the above passage?

A. The most numerous type of Family Court proceeding is juvenile delinquency proceedings.

B. A person of the age of 16 cannot be found by the court to be a juvenile delinquent.

C. If the court finds that a person is a juvenile delinquent, then it must make an order.

D. Family Court handles juvenile delinquency proceedings.

----

51. According to the above passage, which of the following statements is correct?

A. A juvenile delinquent may be of the age of 16.

B. A person over 16 years of age cannot be convicted of a crime.

C. The Family court handles only one type of proceeding.

D. The court may find that a person needs supervision.

For questions 52-53, read the following passage and then answer the questions based solely on the information provided in the passage.

In some states, there are Small Claims Courts which handle cases where the amount sued for does not exceed some small amount, such as $5,000.00. Although most Small Claims cases are scheduled for the evening court session, some cases, including those where one of the parties is over the age of 65 or disabled, are scheduled for the 9:30 AM calendar. These "day" Small Claims cases are tried by a Judge. The "evening" Small Claims cases may be tried by a Judge or arbitrator. Trial by arbitrator is by the prior consent of both parties. Cases tried by a Judge are appealable. However, cases tried by an arbitrator are not appealable since by consenting to arbitration the parties waive their right to appeal.

52.According to the above paragraph:

A. Most Small Claims cases are scheduled for the 9:30 AM calendar call.

B. Arbitrators try some cases scheduled for 9:30 AM.

C. Parties must agree to arbitration before an arbitrator can try their cases.

D. Cases tried by an arbitrator are appealable.

----

53. Which of the following statements is not correct?

A. Cases tried by a Judge are not appealable.

B. Most Small Claims cases are scheduled for the evening court session.

C. Judges and arbitrators may try evening Small Claims cases.

D. Judges try the day Small Claims cases.

For questions 54-55, read the following passage and then answer the questions based solely on the information provided in the passage.

Arraignment is the process by which a criminal court acquires personal jurisdiction over a defendant (a person charged with having committed a criminal offense). A person arrested for allegedly committing a felony is first arraigned in one of the lower criminal courts. If the case is not disposed of at arraignment, the person's future attendance is secured and the case is transferred to the grand jury. A grand jury is a body of 16 to 23 citizens who review the charges and decide whether or not to order the filing of an indictment. The filing of an indictment is a requirement for the prosecution of the felony in one of the superior criminal courts.

54.According to the above passage:

A. An indictment is necessary to prosecute any criminal offense.

B. A person who is charged with committing a felony must first be arraigned in a civil court.

C. A grand jury may consist of 17 persons.

D. An indictment is necessary to prosecute a petty offense in a superior court.

----

55. Which of the following statements is correct?

A. A grand jury may consist of 24 persons.

B. An indictment is a requirement for the prosecution of a felony.

C. A grand jury is prohibited from reviewing charges to decide whether or not to order the filing of an indictment.

D. The lower court cannot arraign a person charged with committing a felony.

For questions 56-60, read the following passage and then answer the questions based solely on the information provided in the passage.

Human Decontamination Procedure

Persons suspected of being contaminated are usually separated by sex, and led into a decontamination tent, trailer, or pod, where they shed their potentially contaminated clothes in a strip-down room. Then they enter a wash-down room where they are showered. Finally, they enter a drying and re-robing room to be issued clean clothing, or a jumpsuit or the like. Some more structured facilities include six rooms (strip-down, wash-down and examination rooms...Facilities, such as Modecs, and many others, are remotely operable, and function like "human car washes". Mass decontamination is the decontamination of large numbers of people. The ACI World Aviation Security Standing Committee describes a decontamination process thus, specifically referring to plans for Los Angeles authorities:

The disinfection/decontamination process is akin to putting humans through a car wash after first destroying their garments. Los Angeles World Airports have put in place a contingency plan to disinfect up to 10,000 persons who might have been exposed to biological or chemical substances.*

-----

56. The above "Human Decontamination Procedure" refers to which type of decontamination?

A. only decontamination of humans exposed to biological substances.

B. only decontamination of humans exposed to chemical substances.

C. decontamination of humans exposed to chemical or biological substances.

D. none of the above

----

57. Which of the following statements is correct?

A. The Los Angeles World Airports have put in place a contingency plan to disinfect up to 1,000 persons who might have been exposed to biological or chemical substances.

B. Modecs, and many others, cannot be operated remotely.

C. Prior to persons being led to a wash-down room, they are usually separated by sex.

D. Some more structured facilities include sixty rooms.

----

58. Which of the following choices is not correct? Persons suspected of being contaminated usually:

A. shed their potentially contaminated clothes in a strip-down room.

B. enter a wash-down room where they are showered.

C. are not separated by sex

D. led into a decontamination tent, trailer, or pod.

----

59. The disinfection/decontamination process is akin to:

A. washing one's hands.

B. brushing one's teeth.

C. putting humans through a car wash.

D. none of the above

----

60. Mass decontamination is:

A. decontamination linked to religious observance.

B. decontamination performed with religious fervor.

C. decontamination done with many decontaminants.

D. decontamination of large numbers of people.

———————

Instructions for Questions 61-105: In the following passages of text, certain words have been deleted and replaced by dashes (one dash for each letter of the word that has been deleted). Using the "contextual clues" in the paragraph, deduce the missing words and record your answers on the answer sheet, as instructed.

Passage 1:

An abandoned vehicle must 61) __ reported to Police Dispatch at 718-555-0105. 62) _ police officer will 63) _ _ assigned to attach a notice on 64) _ _ _ vehicle instructing the owner to remove the vehicle within 48 hours. If the vehicle is 65) _ _ _ removed within 72 hours, the same officer who reported the abandoned vehicle will complete an AVR (Abandoned Vehicle Information) form 66) _ _ _ submit it to the precinct (VR Office). The VR office will assign the report 67) _ _ incident report number and e-mail it to the city Department 68) _ _ Environmental Hazards. If the vehicle is 69) _ _ _ removed within 48 hours, the Department of Environmental Hazards will tow the vehicle to the Waste Metal Recovery Site located in 70) _ _ _ county.

Passage 2:

The term "jail" is often used to refer to an institution 71) _ _ _ _ _ offenders 72) _ _ _ incarcerated for relatively short periods 73) _ _ time. The term "prison" is generally used when the period of incarceration is 74) _ _ _ longer periods. 75) _ _ the United States, jails and prisons are used to incarcerate criminal offenders. However, in some countries they 76) _ _ _ used to imprison social, religious, and political offenders. Although local jurisdictions have a large say 77) _ _ the operation of their jails 78) _ _ _ prisons, all must 79) _ _ Constitutional and all must meet federal standards.

Passage 3:

The duties of police officers vary, depending 80) _ _ the geographical jurisdiction 81) _ _ _ geographic area. Officers 82) _ _ _ usually the first responders to the scene of a crime. 83) _ _ _ _ investigate 84) _ _ _ bring offenders to justice. When not dealing 85) _ _ _ _ criminal activities, 86) _ _ _ _ _ _ officers usually concentrate 87) _ _ keeping the peace and the protection of people 88) _ _ _ property. Because of the stresses of 89) _ _ _ job, police officers usually have liberal sick time leave and generous pension benefits. Also, because of the pride and the benefits of the job, it is common to see more than 90) _ _ _ generation of a family serving 91) _ _ police officers at 92) _ _ _ same time.

Passage 4:

In the United States, public pension plans gained popularity during World War II, a period 93) _ _ _ _ wage freezes prohibited increases 94) _ _ pay. Pensions also gained popularity 95) _ _ many other countries. However, because 96) _ _ recent economic downtrends, increase in 97) _ _ _ _ expectancies, and more liberal medical 98) _ _ _ welfare costs, many countries 99) _ _ _ experiencing 100) _ _ _ possibility 101) _ _ funds shortages 102) _ _ _ even bankruptcy. 103) _ _ keep pension funds solvent, many countries 104) _ _ _ considering revising the age at which workers may retire 105) _ _ _ _ a full pension.

————————

Directions for Questions 106-110: In each of the following five questions, there is a number series. For each number series, you are to figure out the pattern in the series and determine what two numbers (represented by dashes) would be the last two numbers in the series.

----

106)   70 40 65 35 60 30 ___ ___.
A) 68, 37   B) 60, 30   C) 55, 25   D) 50, 20

----

107)   65 69 73 77 81 85 __ __
A) 81, 87   B) 89, 91   C) 87, 93   D) 89, 93

----

108)   1 2 4 8 ___ ___

A) 16, 32   B) 80, 243   C) 8, 32   D) 32, 64

----

109)   30 30 34 34 38 38 42 42 __ __

A) 46, 46   B) 47, 47   C) 48, 48   D) 46, 47

----

110)   93 84 76 69 63 58 __ __

A) 53, 51   B) 54, 51   C) 54, 52   D) 52, 53

Directions: For questions 111-115, select the choice containing the word that does not belong in the group of the other three related words.

Question 111:

A. sympathy

B. awareness

C. feeling

D. bruise

Question 112:

A. site

B. locale

C. place

D. idea

Question 113:

A. undergarment

B. bra

C. jacket

D. briefs

Question 114:

A. priest

B. rabbi

C. bishop

D. relic

Question 115:

A. employee

B. laborer

C. artisan

D. hammer

Question 116

An illegal horde of whiskey bottles was discovered in the suspect's warehouse: 102 bottles of Hutchinson Brand whiskey (80 proof), 346 bottles of Taylor Brand whiskey (78 proof), 164 bottles of Carlton Brand whiskey (88 proof), and 280 bottles of Weyner Brand whiskey (90 proof). What is the name of the brand that contained the third highest proof whiskey?

A. Weyner

B. Carlton

C. Taylor Brand

D. Hutchinson Brand

Question 117

Your sergeant gives you five "Complaint Forms" with the following priority numbers:

4874   21629   0893   976   7892

He asks you to organize the forms in ascending priority.

According to the above, the third Complaint Form would be Complaint Form number:

A. 4874   C. 7892

B. 0893   D. 976

Question 118

Your sergeant gives you five "Requests for Investigation" forms submitted by residents in your precinct. The forms were submitted by the following five persons:

CALIFORNIA POST EXAM GUIDE (PELLETB)

1) Alvin Rutherford, 2) Wanda Jenkins, 3) Carol Chin, 4) Ben Morales, 5) Brenda Hyjek

He asks you to organize the forms in last name alphabetical order.

According to the above, the fourth "Request for Investigation" form is the one submitted by:

A. Hyjek, Brenda

B. Morales, Ben

C. Jenkins, Wanda

D. Branson, Dina

Directions for Questions 119-120: The following 2 questions are comprised of a series of sentences which are in scrambled order. Select the order of sentences (A, B, C, or D) which most correctly and logically places the sentences in a meaningful, logical, and effective order.

Question 119:

1. If you belong to this group, you must have proper documentation.

2. The announcement also contains information regarding fee waiver.

3. A filing fee is required for this examination.

4. Persons receiving Supplemental Social Security benefits are among those persons exempted from the fee.

5. The amount is noted on the examination announcement.

(A) 5-3-4-2-1

(B) 3-5-2-4-1

(C) 3-2-5-4-1

(D) 3-5-2-1-4

Question 120 Organize the following four sentences in the best logical order:

1. State employees receive 20 days of paid vacation during their first year of service, in addition to 12 paid holidays.

2. The total of all these three types of benefit days is 55.

3. The State offers many types of benefits to its employees.

4. They also accrue 13 days of paid annual sick leave.

5. In addition to retirement benefits, it offers three types of paid days.

(A) 5-3-1-2-4

(B) 3-5-1-2-4

(C) 5-3-2-4-2

(D) 3-5-1-4-2

PRACTICE TEST #1 ANSWERS

12

Instructions: For questions 1–15, select the choice with the correct spelling of the omitted word in the preceding sentence.

1. The officer told the teenager that his behavior was not _____.

A. aceptible

B. acceptable

C. acceptabel

D. acceptibel

-----

2. Marking appointments on the _____ is a good way to be reminded of them.

A. callander

B. calender

C. callender

D. calendar

-----

3. Based on the evidence, the jury did not _____ that he was guilty.

A. believe

B. beleve

C. belive

D. beleive

-----

4. He scheduled his vacation during the month of _____.

A. Agoust

B. Augost

C. Augest

D. August

-----

5. They arrived and found him _____.

A. unconscious

B. unconcious

C. unconscius

D. unconcious

-----

6. She was _____ by him because he looked like an honest person.

A. decieved

B. deceived

C. dicieved

D. diceived

---

7. They concluded that he _____ committed the act.

A. definately

B. definitly

C. deffinately

D. definitely

-----

8. His confession placed her in a _____.

A. dilema

B. dilemma

C. delema

D. dealemma

-----

9. The cracks in the door frame indicated _____ entry.

A. forcibele

B. forcible

C. forceable

D. forcable

-----

10. The coroner found a _____ object in her shoulder blade.

A. foreign

B. forriegn

C. forreign

D. foriegn

-----

11. There is no _____ that the search will yield any results.

A. garantee

B. garanty

C.garentee

D. guarantee

-----

12. CIA _____ has found that he is a menber of a terrorist cell.

A. intelegence

B. intelligence

C. intligence

D. intellegence

-----

13. The two robbers are holding three hostages in back of the _____ store

A. juelry

B. jewelry

C. jewellery

D. jewelery

-----

14. The _____ child broke the window by mistake.

A. mischeivous

B. mischevous

C. mischevious

D. mischievous

-----

15. He apologized for the _____ in his report.

A. ommission

B. omision

C. omission

D. ommision

Instructions: For questions 16-30, choose the word that is closest in meaning to the underlined word in the sentence.

16. The sergeant asked the crowd to <u>disperse</u>.

A. gather

B. assemble

C. congregate

D. scatter (Scatter is similar to disperse, spread, disband.)

-----

17. The novice criminal wanted to <u>emulate</u> his senior partner.

A. condemn

B. jostle

C. imitate (Imitate is similar to emulate, mimic, copy.)

D. deride

-----

18. Because of the medication, his motions were <u>erratic</u>.

A. irregular (Irregular is similar to erratic, unpredictable, unstable.)

B. predictable

C. ordinary

D. consistent

-----

19. He said he stole the bags of cookies because he was <u>famished</u>.

A. stuffed

B. starving (Starving is similar to famished, hungry, ravenous.)

C. satiated

D. satisfied

-----

20. He was guilty of conducting an <u>illicit</u> affair.

A. legal

B. proper

C. legitimate

D. illegal (Illegal is similar to illicit, unlawful, criminal.)

-----

21. His actions were <u>incriminating</u>.

A. absolving

B. exonerating

C. damning (Damning is similar to incriminating, accusatory, inculpatory.)

D. clearing

-----

22. The <u>incursion</u> of the gang into the other gang's territory was the reason for the gang war.

A. intrusion (Intrusion is similar to incursion, invasion, penetration.)

B. departure

C. exit

D. egress

-----

23. His constant lying eliminated the possibility of any credulity.

A. trust (Trust is similar to credulity, acceptance, confidence.)

B. disbelief

C. suspicion

D. mistrust

-----

24. The house was small and <u>dilapidated</u>.

A. undamaged

B. shabby (Shabby is similar to decayed, rickety, ramshackle.)

C. mended

D. intact

-----

25. The license plate was so far away that the numbers were not <u>discernable</u>.

A. unclear

B. invisible

C. distinguishable (Distinguishable is similar to discernable, clear, conspicuous.)

D. unperceivable

-----

26. The statements that he made were all <u>fictitious</u>.

A. real

B. true

C. genuine

D. unreal (Unreal is similar to fictitious, false, fanciful.)

-----

27. After examining the door, it was clear that the entry had been <u>forcible</u>.

A. violent (Violent is similar to forcible, aggressive, severe.)

B. forceless

C. weak

D. delicate

-----

28. Only one of the rooms was <u>inhabited</u>.

A. deserted

B. abandoned

C. forsaken

D. occupied (Occupied is similar to inhabited, populated, tenanted.)

-----

29. It was a <u>malicious</u> attempt to destroy her credibility.

A. kind

B. benevolent

C. wicked (Wicked is similar to malicious, mean, nasty.)

D. benign

-----

30. The <u>prescription</u> vial lay on the table.

A. drug (Drug is similar to prescription, medicine.)

B. poison

C. liquid

D. premium

CALIFORNIA POST EXAM GUIDE (PELLETB)

Instructions: For the following questions 15 questions, (Questions 31-45), decide which sentence is most clearly written.

Choose "A" if sentence "a" is clearer than sentence "b".
Choose "B" if sentence "b" is clearer than sentence "a".

Question 31:

a. Spotting the gunman behind the crates, his heart beat faster.

b. When he spotted the gunman behind the crates, the officer's heart beat faster.

Answer 1: B (Sentence "a" does not make clear whose heart beat faster.)

Question 32:

a. Even the officers who were tired took turns at guard duty.

b. The officers took turns at guard duty. Even the officers that were tired.

Answer 2: A ("b" contains a sentence fragment, ("Even the officers that were tired."))

Question 33:

a. The bank manager thanked the officer for searching for his missing gun.

b. The bank manager thanked the officer for searching for the bank manager's missing gun.

Answer 33: B ("a" is confusing because it is not clear whose gun is missing. The "his" in "his missing gun" does not make it clear whose gun is missing.)

Question 34:

a. Feeling very frightened, the throat dried up.

b. Because the officer was feeling frightened, the officer's throat dried up.

Answer: B ("a" is unclear as to whose throat dried up.)

Question 35:

a. Aided by the four teenagers, the officer was able to carry the chest.

b. The officer was able to carry the chest. Aided by the four teenagers.

Answer 35: A ("b" contains the sentence fragment, "Aided by the four teenagers.")

Question 36:

a. The demonstrators marched in the street, the police officers walked on the sidewalk.

b. The demonstrators marched in the street. The police officers walked on the sidewalk.

Answer 36: B ("a" is a run-on sentence.)

Question 37:

a. Trying to avoid the rocks, the truck offered a good shield.

b. Trying to avoid the rocks, the officer used the truck as a shield.

Answer 37: B ("a" contains a modification error. It makes it seem like the truck was trying to avoid the rocks.)

Question 38:

a. The witness liked the attorney as did the D.A.

b. The witness liked the attorney as much as the D.A.

Answer 38: B ("a" is not clear as to whom the witness likes - the attorney, D.A., or both?)

Question 39:

a. After the officer and the rioter fought, the officer's finger started bleeding.

b. After the officer fought with the rioter, his finger started bleeding.

Answer 39: A ("b" contains a reference error. It is not clear who "his" is referring to.)

Question 40:

a. The squad radio was malfunctioning every day. It needed to be repaired.

b. The squad radio was malfunctioning every day, it needed to be repaired.

Answer 40: A ("b" is a run-on sentence.)

Question 41:

a. Blowing out black fumes, Officer Carlton turned off the emergency switch.

b. Because the furnace was blowing out black fumes, Officer Carlton turned off the emergency switch.

Answer 41: B ("a" has a modification error. It is unclear what is blowing out black fumes - Officer Carlton, or the furnace?)

Question 42:

a. The work shift was long and tiresome, especially the last two hours.

b. The work shift was long and tiresome. Especially the last two hours.

Answer 42: A ("b" contains the sentence fragment, "Especially the last two hours.")

Question 43:

a. Because his uniform was stained by the red rioter's paint, he had it dry cleaned.

b. Because his uniform was stained by the rioter's red paint, he had it dry cleaned.

Answer 43: B ('a" is clumsy. "the rioter's red paint" is smoother and not clumsy, as is the phrase "red rioter's paint.")

Question 44:

a. He ate cookies and drank soda. Waiting for his mother to pick him up.

b. While waiting for his mother to pick him up, he ate cookies and drank soda.

Answer 44: B ("a" contains the sentence fragment, " Waiting for his mother to pick him up.")

Question 45:

a. After placing the evidence in the envelope, he took it to his squad car.

b. After placing the evidence in the envelope, he took the envelope to his squad car.

Answer 45: B ("a" has a reference error. It does not make clear what specifically was carried to the squad car.)

For questions 46-47, read the following passage and then answer the questions based solely on the information provided in the passage.

There is a county court in each county outside the capital city. The county court has limited jurisdiction in civil cases. It may try cases where the amount sued for does not exceed $25,000.00. The county court is also authorized to handle the prosecution of crimes that have been committed inside the county. To lessen the administrative burden posed by the arraignment and preliminary proceedings in numerous criminal cases, courts of limited jurisdiction lower than that of the county court usually handle these initial steps in the criminal prosecution process.

-----

46. Which of the following statements is supported by the above paragraph?

A. The county court in a capital city has a maximum jurisdiction of $25,000.00.

B. County Courts do not handle the initial steps in the criminal prosecution process.

C. Arraignments are handled by the San Francisco Supreme Court.

D. County courts handle both civil and criminal cases within their jurisdiction.

----

47. Which of the following statements is not correct?

A. The capital city does not have a county court.

B. The county court is authorized to handle the prosecution of crimes committed outside the county.

C. The county court can handle some civil cases.

D. The county court can try cases where the amount sued for is $10,000.

For questions 48-49, read the following passage and then answer the questions based solely on the information provided in the passage.

Felonies are the highest type of crimes. The other category of crimes, misdemeanors, are crimes which expose the perpetrator to jail terms which are less than those imposed for felonies. For example, the highest term of imprisonment that can be imposed for a misdemeanor conviction is one year. Felonies can subject the perpetrator to imprisonment of up to life imprisonment or even death.

-----

48. Which of the following statements is supported by the above passage?

A. Jostling in the first degree is a felony.

B. "A" misdemeanors are more severe than "B" misdemeanors.

C. Misdemeanors are crimes of greater severity than petty offenses.

D. Misdemeanors and felonies are crimes.

----

49. Which of the following statements is not correct?

A. Felonies are crimes.

B. A misdemeanor prison sentence may be for a one year term.

C. Imprisonment for a felony must be for less than a year.

D. A sentence for a felony may be death.

For questions 50-51, read the following passage and then answer the questions based solely on the information provided in the passage.

Family Court handles different types of proceedings. One of the most numerous type of proceeding is juvenile delinquency proceedings. A juvenile delinquent is defined as a person over the age of 7 and less than 15 who commits an act which would be a crime if the person were over the age of 15. After a fact-finding hearing, if the court finds that the person committed the act, and if it also finds that the person needs supervision, treatment or confinement, then the court must find that the person is a juvenile delinquent and must make an order prescribing the required supervision, treatment or confinement.

-----

50. Which of the following statements is not correct as per the above passage?

A. The most numerous type of Family Court proceeding is juvenile delinquency proceedings.

B. A person of the age of 16 cannot be found by the court to be a juvenile delinquent.

C. If the court finds that a person is a juvenile delinquent, then it must make an order.

D. Family Court handles juvenile delinquency proceedings.

----

51. According to the above passage, which of the following statements is correct?

A. A juvenile delinquent may be of the age of 16.

B. A person over 16 years of age cannot be convicted of a crime.

C. The Family court handles only one type of proceeding.

D. The court may find that a person needs supervision.

For questions 52-53, read the following passage and then answer the questions based solely on the information provided in the passage.

In some states, there are Small Claims Courts which handle cases where the amount sued for does not exceed some small amount, such as $5,000.00. Although most Small Claims cases are scheduled for the evening court session, some cases, including those where one of the parties is over the age of 65 or disabled, are scheduled for the 9:30 AM calendar. These "day" Small Claims cases are tried by a Judge. The "evening" Small Claims cases may be tried by a Judge or arbitrator. Trial by arbitrator is by the prior consent of both parties. Cases tried by a Judge are appealable. However, cases tried by an arbitrator are not appealable since by consenting to arbitration the parties waive their right to appeal.

-----

52. According to the above paragraph:

A. Most Small Claims cases are scheduled for the 9:30 AM calendar call.

B. Arbitrators try some cases scheduled for 9:30 AM.

C. Parties must agree to arbitration before an arbitrator can try their cases.

D. Cases tried by an arbitrator are appealable.

----

53. Which of the following statements is not correct?

A. Cases tried by a Judge are not appealable.

B. Most Small Claims cases are scheduled for the evening court session.

C. Judges and arbitrators may try evening Small Claims cases.

D. Judges try the day Small Claims cases.

For questions 54-55, read the following passage and then answer the questions based solely on the information provided in the passage.

Arraignment is the process by which a criminal court acquires personal jurisdiction over a defendant (a person charged with having committed a criminal offense). A person arrested for allegedly committing a felony is first arraigned in one of the lower criminal courts. If the case is not disposed of at arraignment, the person's future attendance is secured and the case is transferred to the grand jury. A grand jury is a body of 16 to 23 citizens who review the charges and decide whether or not to order the filing of an indictment. The filing of an indictment is a requirement for the prosecution of the felony in one of the superior criminal courts.

-----

54. According to the above passage:

A. An indictment is necessary to prosecute any criminal offense.

B. A person who is charged with committing a felony must first be arraigned in a civil court.

C. A grand jury may consist of 17 persons.

D. An indictment is necessary to prosecute a petty offense in a superior court.

----

55. Which of the following statements is correct?

A. A grand jury may consist of 24 persons.

B. An indictment is a requirement for the prosecution of a felony.

C. A grand jury is prohibited from reviewing charges to decide whether or not to order the filing of an indictment.

D. The lower court cannot arraign a person charged with committing a felony.

For questions 56-60, read the following passage and then answer the questions based solely on the information provided in the passage.

Human Decontamination Procedure

Persons suspected of being contaminated are usually separated by sex, and led into a decontamination tent, trailer, or pod, where they shed their potentially contaminated clothes in a strip-down room. Then they enter a wash-down room where they are showered. Finally, they enter a drying and re-robing room to be issued clean clothing, or a jumpsuit or the like. Some more structured facilities include six rooms (strip-down, wash-down and examination rooms...Facilities, such as Modecs, and many others, are remotely operable, and function like "human car washes". Mass decontamination is the decontamination of large numbers of people. The ACI World Aviation Security Standing Committee describes a decontamination process thus, specifically referring to plans for Los Angeles authorities:

The disinfection/decontamination process is akin to putting humans through a car wash after first destroying their garments. Los Angeles World Airports have put in place a contingency plan to disinfect up to 10,000 persons who might have been exposed to biological or chemical substances.*

-----

56. The above "Human Decontamination Procedure" refers to which type of decontamination?

A. only decontamination of humans exposed to biological substances.

B. only decontamination of humans exposed to chemical substances.

C. decontamination of humans exposed to chemical or biological substances.

(THIS IS THE ANSWER. "The ACI World Aviation Security Standing Committee describes a decontamination process thus...who might have been exposed to biological or chemical substances.")

D. none of the above

----

57. Which of the following statements is correct?

A. The Los Angeles World Airports have put in place a contingency plan to disinfect up to 1,000 persons who might have been exposed to biological or chemical substances.

(**NOT CORRECT**. The number of person is 10,000 and not 1,000.)

B. Modecs, and many others, cannot be operated remotely.

(**NOT CORRECT**. "Modecs, and many others, are remotely operable, and function like "human car washes.")

C. Prior to persons being led to a wash-down room, they are usually separated by sex.

(**CORRECT**. "Persons suspected of being contaminated are usually separated by sex, and led into a decontamination tent, trailer, or pod, where they shed their potentially contaminated clothes in a strip-down room. Then they enter a wash-down room where they are showered.")

D. Some more structured facilities include sixty rooms.

(**NOT CORRECT**. Correct number of rooms is **six**.)

----

58. Which of the following choices is not correct? Persons suspected of being contaminated usually:

A. shed their potentially contaminated clothes in a strip-down room.

B. enter a wash-down room where they are showered.

C. are not separated by sex

D. led into a decontamination tent, trailer, or pod.

----

59. The disinfection/decontamination process is akin to:

A. washing one's hands.

B. brushing one's teeth.

C. putting humans through a car wash.

D. none of the above

----

60. Mass decontamination is:

A. decontamination linked to religious observance.

B. decontamination performed with religious fervor.

C. decontamination done with many decontaminants.

D. decontamination of large numbers of people.

Instructions for Questions 61-105: In the following passages of text, certain words have been deleted and replaced by dashes (one dash for each letter of the word that has

been deleted). Using the "contextual clues" in the paragraph, deduce the missing words and record your answers on the answer sheet, as instructed.

Passage 1:

An abandoned vehicle must 61) __ reported to Police Dispatch at 718-555-0105. 62) _ police officer will 63) _ _ assigned to attach a notice on 64) _ _ _ vehicle instructing the owner to remove the vehicle within 48 hours. If the vehicle is 65) _ _ _ removed within 72 hours, the same officer who reported the abandoned vehicle will complete an AVR (Abandoned Vehicle Information) form 66) _ _ _ submit it to the precinct (VR Office). The VR office will assign the report 67) _ _ incident report number and e-mail it to the city Department 68) _ _ Environmental Hazards. If the vehicle is 69) _ _ _ removed within 48 hours, the Department of Environmental Hazards will tow the vehicle to the Waste Metal Recovery Site located in 70) _ _ _ county.

Passage 2:

The term "jail" is often used to refer to an institution 71) _ _ _ _ _ offenders 72) _ _ _ incarcerated for relatively short periods 73) _ _ time. The term "prison" is generally used when the period of incarceration is 74) _ _ _ longer periods. 75) _ _ the United States, jails and prisons are used to incarcerate criminal offenders. However, in some countries they 76) _ _ _ used to imprison social, religious, and political offenders. Although local jurisdictions have a large say 77) _ _ the operation of their jails 78) _ _ _ prisons, all must 79) _ _ Constitutional and all must meet federal standards.

Passage 3:

The duties of police officers vary, depending 80) _ _ the geographical jurisdiction 81) _ _ _ geographic area. Officers 82) _ _ _ usually the first responders to the scene of a crime. 83) _ _ _ _ investigate 84) _ _ _ bring offenders to justice. When not dealing 85) _ _ _ _ criminal activities, 86) _ _ _ _ _ _ officers usually concentrate 87) _ _ keeping the peace and the protection of people 88) _ _ _ property. Because of the stresses of 89) _ _ _ job, police officers usually have liberal sick time leave and generous pension benefits. Also, because of the pride and the benefits of the job, it is common to see more than 90) _ _ _ generation of a family serving 91) _ _ police officers at 92) _ _ _ same time.

Passage 4:

In the United States, public pension plans gained popularity during World War II, a period 93) _ _ _ _ wage freezes prohibited increases 94) _ _ pay. Pensions also gained popularity 95) _ _ many other countries. However, because 96) _ _ recent economic downtrends, increase in 97) _ _ _ _ expectancies, and more liberal medical 98) _ _ _ welfare costs, many countries 99) _ _ _ experiencing 100) _ _ _ possibility 101) _ _ funds shortages 102) _ _ _ even bankruptcy. 103) _ _ keep pension funds solvent, many countries 104) _ _ _ considering revising the age at which workers may retire 105) _ _ _ _ a full pension.

Answer for Questions 61-105:

61. be	76. are	91. as
62. a	77. in	92. the
63. be	78. and	93. when
64. the	79. be	94. in
65. not	80. on	95. in
66. and	81. and	96. of
67. an	82. are	97. life
68. of	83. they	98. and
69. not	84. and	99. are
70. the	85. with	100. the
71. where	86. police	101. of
72. are	87. on	102. and
73. of	88. and	103. to
74. for	89. the	104. are
75. in	90. one	105. with

Directions for Questions 106-110: In each of the following five questions, there is a number series. For each number series, you are to figure out the pattern in the series and determine what two numbers (represented by dashes) would be the last two numbers in the series.

----

106)　　　70　40　65　35　60　30　___ ___.

A) 68, 37　　　　B) 60, 30　　　　C) 55, 25　　　　D) 50, 20

Answer 106: C (55, 25)

Pattern is two DOUBLE numbers (70 and 40) ALTERNATING and DECREASING by 5 each time.

----

107)　　　65　69　73　77　81　85　__ __

A) 81, 87　　　　B) 89, 91　　　　C) 87, 93　　　　D) 89, 93

Answer 107: D (89, 93)

Pattern is the number 65 INCREASING by 4 each time the pattern is repeated.

----

108)　　　1　2　4　8　___ ___

A) 16, 32　　　　B) 80, 243　　　　C) 8, 32　　　　D) 32, 64

Answer 108: A (16, 32)

Pattern is 1 MULTIPLIED by 2 each time the pattern is repeated (1 X 2 = 2, 2 X 2 = 4, 4 X 2 = 8, 8 X 2 = 16, 16 X 2 = 32).

----

109)　　　30　30　34　34　38　38　42　42　__ __

A) 46, 46　　　　B) 47, 47　　　　C) 48, 48　　　　D) 46, 47

Answer 109: A (46, 46)

The pattern is the number 30 REPEATED once and then INCREASED by 4 each time the pattern is repeated (30, Repeat 30, 30 + 4 = 34, Repeat 34, 34 + 4 = 38, Repeat 38, 38 + 4 = 42, Repeat 42, 42 + 4 = 46, Repeat 46).

----

110)   93 84 76 69 63 58 __ __

A) 53, 51   B) 54, 51   C) 54, 52   D) 52, 53

Answer 110: B (54, 51)

The pattern is the number 93 DECREASING by a DECREASING number each time the pattern is repeated (93 - 9 = 84, 84 - 8 = 76, 76 - 7 = 69, 69 - 6 = 63, 63 - 5 = 58, 58 - 4 = 54, 54 - 3 = 51).

Directions: For questions 111-115, select the choice containing the word that does not belong in the group of the other three related words.

Question 111:

A. sympathy

B. awareness

C. feeling

D. bruise (The other 3 words relate to feelings. Bruise is a physical injury.)

Question 112:

A. site

B. locale

C. place

D. idea (The other 3 words refer to locations. Idea refers to a thought process.)

Question 113:

A. undergarment

B. bra

C. jacket (The other 3 words are items are undergarments. Jacket is worn as an outer layer of clothing.)

D. briefs

Question 114:

A. priest

B. rabbi

C. bishop

D. relic (The other 3 words are religious titles. Relic is an object.)

Question 115:

A. employee

B. laborer

C. artisan

D. hammer (The other 3 words relate to people. Hammer is an object.)

Question 116

An illegal horde of whiskey bottles was discovered in the suspect's warehouse: 102 bottles of Hutchinson Brand whiskey (80 proof), 346 bottles of Taylor Brand whiskey (78 proof), 164 bottles of Carlton Brand whiskey (88 proof), and 280 bottles of Weyner Brand whiskey (90 proof). What is the name of the brand that contained the third highest proof whiskey?

A. Weyner

B. Carlton

(The order, according to the "proof", is: 1) Taylor Brand (78 proof), 2) Hutchinson Brand (80 proof), 3) Carlton Brand (88 proof), and 4) Weyner Brand (90 proof).)

C. Taylor Brand

D. Hutchinson Brand

Question 117

Your sergeant gives you five "Complaint Forms" with the following priority numbers:

4874   21629   0893   976   7892

He asks you to organize the forms in ascending priority.

According to the above, the third Complaint Form would be Complaint Form number:

A. 4874   C. 7892

B. 0893   D. 976

The Complaint Forms in Ascending Priority Number Order are as follows:

1) 0893

2) 976

3) 4874

4) 7892

5) 21629

The third complaint number on the list is **4874**. Therefore, the correct answer is **A) 4874**.

Question 118

Your sergeant gives you five "Requests for Investigation" forms submitted by residents in your precinct. The forms were submitted by the following five persons:

1) Alvin Rutherford, 2) Wanda Jenkins, 3) Carol Chin, 4) Ben Morales, 5) Brenda Hyjek

He asks you to organize the forms in last name alphabetical order.

According to the above, the fourth "Request for Investigation" form is the one submitted by:

A. Hyjek, Brenda

B. Morales, Ben

C. Jenkins, Wanda

D. Branson, Dina

Answer 118

The correct listing in <u>last name alphabetical order</u> is:

1) Chin, Carol

2) Hyjek, Brenda

3) Jenkins, Wanda

4) Morales, Ben

5) Rutherford, Alvin

The fourth name on the list is Morales, Ben, therefore the correct answer is **B. Morales, Ben**.

Directions for Questions 119-120: The following 2 questions are comprised of a series of sentences which are in scrambled order. Select the order of sentences (A, B, C, or D) which most correctly and logically places the sentences in a meaningful, logical, and effective order.

Question 119:

1. If you belong to this group, you must have proper documentation.

2. The announcement also contains information regarding fee waiver.

3. A filing fee is required for this examination.

4. Persons receiving Supplemental Social Security benefits are among those persons exempted from the fee.

5. The amount is noted on the examination announcement.

(A) 5-3-4-2-1

(B) 3-5-2-4-1

(C) 3-2-5-4-1

(D) 3-5-2-1-4

Answer 119: (B) 3-5-2-4-1

(3) A filing fee is required for this examination.

(5) The amount is noted on the examination announcement.

(2) The announcement also contains information regarding fee waiver.

(4) Persons receiving Supplemental Social Security benefits are among those persons exempted from the fee.

(1) If you belong to this group, you must have proper documentation.

Question 120 Organize the following four sentences in the best logical order:

1. State employees receive 20 days of paid vacation during their first year of service, in addition to 12 paid holidays.

2. The total of all these three types of benefit days is 55.

3. The State offers many types of benefits to its employees.

4. They also accrue 13 days of paid annual sick leave.

5. In addition to retirement benefits, it offers three types of paid days.

(A) 5-3-1-2-4

(B) 3-5-1-2-4

(C) 5-3-2-4-2

(D) 3-5-1-4-2

Answer 1:   (D) 3-5-1-4-2

(3) The State offers many types of benefits to its employees.

(5) In addition to retirement benefits, it offers three types of paid days.

(1) State employees receive 20 days of paid vacation during their first year of service, in addition to 12 paid holidays

(4) They also accrue 13 days of paid annual sick leave.

(2) The total of all these three types of benefit days is 55 days.

PRACTICE TEST #2 QUESTIONS | 13

Instructions: For questions 1–15, select the choice with the correct spelling of the omitted word in the preceding sentence.

1. The lineup is scheduled for _____.

A. Tuesdey

B. Tusday

C. Tuesday

D. Teusday

-----

2. The _____ distributed a copy of the map to all the officers.

A. sargeant

B. sargent

C. sergant

D. sergeant

-----

3. The informant said that the suspect eats at the _____ on Friday nights.

A. restaurant

B. restorant

C. restarant

D. resterant

-----

4. She knew all the details because she was the _____ of the social club.

A. secratary

B. secretery

C. secritery

D. secretary

-----

5. In addition to being a mob boss, he was a _____ businessman.

A. successfull

B. sucsesful

C. successful

D. succeful

-----

6. The Captain said that this directive _____ the one issued last year.

A. supercedes

B. superceedes

C. superceeds

D. suppercedes

-----

7. Everyone was_____ by his quick confession.

A. supprised

B. surprised

C. suprised

D. surrprised

-----

8. He used the _____ cleaner cord to strangle him.

A. vaccuum

B. vacume

C. vaccume

D. vacuum

-----

9. The _____ agency reported the signs of child abuse.

A. wellfare

B. welfare

C. welfere

D. welfair

-----

10. Before he left, he conducted a _____ search.

A. thorough

B. thorugh

C. thorrow

D. thourogh

-----

11. The hostage taker announced that he wanted to make a _____ to the world.

A. speach

B. spiech

C. speech

D. speich

-----

12. The judge stated that the evidence was not _____ to the case.

A. relevant

B. relevent

C. rellevant

D. revelant

-----

13. He announced that he would not take his hat off in the courtroom because of _____

reasons.

A. religous

B. relligious

C. relligous

D. religious

-----

14. He said he would not pay the ticket on _____.

A. principal

B. principle

C. principel

D. princeple

-----

15. He was found guilty of _____ of heroin.

A. possesion

B. possession

C. posesion

D. posession

Instructions: **For questions 16-30, choose the word that is closest in meaning to the underlined word in the sentence.**

16. Although he stated that he wasn't fighting, the suspect looked underlined{disheveled}.

A. clean

B. neat

C. unwrinkled

D. ruffled

-----

17. He tried to extort a large sum of money from the bank.

A. offer

B. give

C. coerce

D. surrender

-----

18. The main reason why he fell for the scam was that he was young and impetuous.

A. cautious

B. impulsive

C. calm

D. considerate

-----

19. Both he and his girlfriend had an irrational fear of riding in a car.

A. responsible

B. logical

C. sensible

D. unreasonable

-----

20. She had no recollection of the car entering the danger zone.

A. vagueness

B. reason

C. memory

D. purpose

-----

21. The handle of the screwdriver was <u>protruding</u> from the car's side door.

A. shrinking

B. extending

C. contracting

D. depressing

-----

22. He saw the <u>silhouette</u> of the suspect in front of the partition.

A. brightness

B. contour

C. light

D. brilliance

-----

23. He used the hose to <u>siphon</u> gas from the gas tank.

A. drain

B. restore

C. return

D. restitute

-----

24. <u>Restitution</u> is often ordered in family court cases.

A. reimbursement

B. dissatisfaction

C. imprisonment

C. parole

-----

25. The attorney made two motions to <u>suppress</u> the introduction of the evidence.

A. allow

B. permit

C. sanction

D. repress

-----

26. His <u>adversary</u> was wearing a red business suit.

A. welcoming

B. hospitable

C. non-antagonistic

D. opponent

-----

27. Because of a lack of evidence, the <u>allegation</u> was not proven.

A. denial

B. accusation

C. disclaim

D. defense

-----

28. The <u>contusion</u> was on his forehead.

A. cure

B. healer

C. bruise

D. treatment

-----

29. His statement was <u>corroborated</u> by two witnesses.

A. contradicted

B. substantiated

C. denied

D. disclaimed

-----

30. He was <u>detained</u> for a few hours.

A. confined

B. liberated

C. released

D. free

CALIFORNIA POST EXAM GUIDE (PELLETB)

Instructions: For the following questions 15 questions, (Questions 31-45), decide which sentence is most clearly written.

Choose "A" if sentence "a" is clearer than sentence "b".
Choose "B" if sentence "b" is clearer than sentence "a".

Question 31:

a. The informant was seated at the table, he was very helpful.

b. The very helpful informant was seated at the table.

Question 32:

a. The victim pointed to the student who looked like the attacker in the class picture.

b. The victim pointed to the student in the class picture who looked like the attacker.

Question 33:

a. The officer instructed the driver to take his driver's license out of his wallet and place it on the seat.

b. The officer instructed the driver to take his driver's license out of his wallet and place the license on the seat.

Question 34:

a. The squad room is very tight, but they use it anyway.

b. The squad room is very tight, but the officers use it anyway.

Question 35:

a. The officer spotted the gold man's watch that was reported stolen.

b. The officer spotted the man's gold watch that was reported stolen.

Question 36:

a. The volunteers took the cookies to the homeless shelter, where they were very much welcomed.

b. The volunteers took the cookies to the homeless shelter. Very much welcomed.

Question 37:

a. The witness threw out the toy, which was a mistake.

b. The witness made the mistake of throwing out the toy.

Question 38:

a. The boxes were scattered in the parking lot. The tools were piled in front of the entrance.

b. The boxes were scattered in the parking lot, the tools were piled in front of the entrance.

Question 39:

a. Because of the "certain look," the gang members realized he had figured out their scheme.

b. Because of the "certain look" from the officer, the gang members realized he had figured out their scheme.

Question 40:

a. The officer picked up the silver dirty pin from the floor.

b. The officer picked up the dirty silver pin from the floor.

Question 41:

a. Seeing the child running away from her attacker, the officer's heart skipped in joy.

b. The officer's heart skipped in joy. Seeing the child running away from her attacker.

Question 42:

a. Even the rookie officers volunteered for overtime duty.

b. The officers volunteered for overtime duty. Even the rookie officers.

Question 43:

a. The store owner thanked the sergeant for finding his missing pepper spray.

b. The store owner thanked the sergeant for finding the store owner's missing pepper spray.

Question 44:

a. Aided by the rookies, the senior officer completed the report on time.

b. The senior officer completed the report on time. Aided by the rookies.

Question 45:

a. The officer put the gun in a box and told the rookie to take it to the evidence room.

b. The officer put the gun in a box and told the rookie to take the box to the evidence room.

_____

For questions 46-47, read the following passage and then answer the questions based solely on the information provided in the passage.

A Police Officer must inform a person that she arrests that the person has the right to remain silent and that anything the person says may be used against the person in a court of law. The arresting officer must also inform the person that the person has the right to speak with an attorney before speaking with the arresting officer and that the person has the right to have an attorney present during questioning, and that if the person cannot afford an attorney, one will be provided by the state.

46.Which of the following statements is correct according to the above paragraph?

A. If an attorney is not present, a Police Officer shall not make an arrest.

B. Statements made by an arrested person may not be used in a court of law.

C. If a person can afford an attorney, the state will provide one.

D. A person may demand that an attorney be present during questioning.

----

47. Which of the following statements is not correct according to the above paragraph?

A. If the person cannot afford an attorney, one will be provided by the state.

B. The person has the right to remain silent.

C. The person must also inform the arresting officer that the person has the right to speak with an attorney before speaking with the arresting officer.

D. The person has the right to have an attorney present during questioning.

For questions 48-49, read the following passage and then answer the questions based solely on the information provided in the passage.

The Americans With Disabilities Act applies to all court buildings, whether they are state owned or owned by private owners. It requires the California Court System to make reasonable accommodations for people with disabilities. In structures completed before January 1, 1994, reasonable accommodations may be made by physical modification of existing structures to meet ADA guidelines or by establishing procedures to otherwise reasonably accommodate people with disabilities. For example, in structures built after January 1, 1994, an entrance ramp must be provided where the first-floor entrance is above street level. In structures built before January 1, 1994 an alternative entrance, such as a back entrance, may be used if it provides access to the building at ground level.

-----

48. According to the above paragraph:

A. All back entrances to buildings must be at ground level.

B. An entrance ramp must be provided in all court buildings built after January 1, 1994.

C. Some ADA requirements do not require physical modification of existing structures.

D. ADA rules apply to all government buildings.

----

49. Which of the following four statements is not correct according to the above passage?

A. The Americans With Disabilities Act applies to all court buildings.

B. In certain structures, reasonable accommodations may be made by physical modification of existing structures to meet ADA guidelines.

C. The Americans With Disabilities Act requires the California Court System to make reasonable accommodations for people with disabilities.

D. In structures built after January 1, 1994 an alternative entrance, such as a back entrance, may be used if it provides access to the building at ground level.

For questions 50-51, read the following passage and then answer the questions based solely on the information provided in the passage.

Although almost all court buildings are air conditioned, in some buildings there are some rooms or areas where the air conditioning system might not always be sufficient. This situation can occur because the power of the air conditioning system might not be adequate for the area, or because the system might need repair. If the temperature in a room rises above 84 degrees, then the employees must be relocated to another room. If there are no areas in the building where the temperature is below 84 degrees, then the employees shall be released with pay for the day. The release of the employees and the resulting suspension of court activity in the building must be prior approved by the head of Facilities, Brian Jenkins. In his absence, Vance Johnson of personnel relations may provide the same approval.

-----

50. According to the above passage, which of the following statements is not correct?

A. Employees working in a room must be relocated if the temperature rises above 84 degrees in the room.

B. If the temperature rises above 84 degrees in all the rooms of a court building, only Vance Johnson may approve the release of employees and suspension of court activity.

C. If employees are relocated to a different room, the temperature in the room to which they are relocated may not be more than 83 degrees.

D. Employees properly released due to excessive temperature do not lose any pay due to the release.

51. According to the preceding paragraph, which of the following statements is correct?

If the temperature in a room rises above 84 degrees, Vance Johnson, head of Facilities.

A. The temperature in a room may never rise above 84 degrees.

B. Vance Johnson is the head of Facilities.

C. Brian Jenkins works in personnel relations.

D. Not all court buildings are air-conditioned.

For questions 52-53, read the following passage and then answer the questions based solely on the information provided in the passage.

Probationary Trainees receive approximately 16 weeks of training at the Probationary Trainees Academy, located at 87 Windham Place. The majority of the training is done in a classroom setting. In the classroom setting trainees receive instruction in such matters as public relations, criminal statutes, court procedures, first aid and crowd control. Training and qualification in the Glock semi-automatic are done at the firing range located at 12 Leonard Street. Following the academy training, Probationary Trainees are assigned to a specific town where they are further trained in the security and clerical procedures of that town. Although Probationary Trainees are primarily responsible for security, knowledge of clerical procedures helps them to better serve the public.

52. According to the above passage, which of the following statements is correct?

A. Training in the Glock semi-automatic is sometimes done at 87 Windham Street.

B. Probationary Trainees are primarily responsible for clerical procedures.

C. The Probationary Trainees Academy lasts approximately 4 weeks.

D. Security is the main responsibility of Probationary Trainees.

----

53. According to the above passage, which of the following statements is not correct?

A. Prior to attending the academy, a Probationary Trainee is assigned to a specific town.

B. The firing range is located at 12 Leonard Street.

C. The Probationary Trainees Academy is located at 87 Windham Place.

D. At the town of assignment, Probationary Trainees are further trained in clerical procedures.

For questions 54-55, read the following passage and then answer the questions based solely on the information provided in the passage.

In certain areas, Landlord and Tenant cases initiated by landlords are separated into two general categories, Non-Payments and Holdovers. Non-Payments seek an order of the court for the tenant to pay the owed rent or be evicted from the premises. Holdovers seek an order requiring the tenant to move and the return of the premises to the landlord. The court fee for filing a Non-Payment or Holdover is $45.00 per case. This is paid to the cashier upon the issuance of an L&T number and must be in cash, certified check or money order made payable to the County Court. The fee for certification of court documents is $6.00. The transcript of judgment fee is $15.00.

-----

54. Which of the following statement is correct according to the above passage?

A. Holdovers seek an order requiring the tenant to pay the owed rent or be evicted from the premises.

B. Non-Payment proceedings are more numerous than Holdover proceedings.

C. The $45.00 filing fee may be paid by check made payable to the County Court.

D. Non-Payment proceedings seek the eviction of the tenant if the owed rent is not paid.

----

55. According to the above passage, which of the following statements is not correct?

A. The fee for certification of court documents is $6.00.

B. Non-Payments seek an order requiring the tenant to move and the return of the premises to the landlord

C. The transcript of judgment fee is $15.00.

D. In some areas, Landlord and Tenant cases initiated by landlords are separated into two general categories, Non-Payments and Holdovers.

For questions 56-60, read the following passage and then answer the questions based solely on the information provided in the passage.

Biohazard Levels

The United States Centers for Disease Control and Prevention (CDC) categorizes various diseases in levels of biohazard, Level 1 being minimum risk and Level 4 being extreme risk.

Biohazard Level 1:

Bacteria and viruses including Bacillus subtilis, canine hepatitis, Escherichia coli, varicella (chicken pox), as well as some cell cultures and non-infectious bacteria. At this level precautions against the biohazardous materials in question are minimal, most likely involving gloves and some sort of facial protection.

Biohazard Level 2:

Bacteria and viruses that cause only mild disease to humans, or are difficult to contract via aerosol in a lab setting, such as hepatitis A, B, and C, influenza A, Lyme disease, salmonella, mumps, measles, scrapie, dengue fever.

Biohazard Level 3:

Bacteria and viruses that can cause severe to fatal disease in humans, but for which vaccines or other treatments exist, such as anthrax, West Nile virus, Venezuelan equine encephalitis, SARS virus, tuberculosis, typhus, Rift Valley fever, HIV, Rocky Mountain spotted fever, yellow fever, and malaria. Among parasites Plasmodium falciparum, which causes Malaria, and Trypanosoma cruzi, which causes trypanosomiasis, also come under this level.

Biohazard Level 4:

Viruses and bacteria that cause severe to fatal disease in humans, and for which vaccines or other treatments are not available, such as Bolivian and Argentine hemorrhagic fevers, Marburg virus, Ebola virus, hantaviruses, Lassa fever virus, Crimean–Congo hemorrhagic fever, and other hemorrhagic diseases. Variola virus (smallpox) is an agent that is worked with at BSL-4 despite the existence of a vaccine. When dealing with biological hazards at this level the use of a positive pressure personnel suit, with a segregated air supply, is mandatory.*

-----

56. According to the preceding "Biohazard Levels" passage, the highest and most dangerous biohazard risk is designated as:

A. Biohazard Level 1

B. Biohazard Level 2

C. Biohazard Level 3

D. Biohazard Level 4

----

57. A "positive pressure personnel suit" must be used when dealing with Biohazard Level(s):

A. Biohazard Level 1 only.

B. Biohazard Levels 1 and 2 only.

C. Biohazard Level 1, 2, 3 and 4.

D. Biohazard Level 4.

----

58. The parasite Plasmodium falciparum, which causes Malaria Malria, comes under Biohazard Level:

A. 1

B. 2

C. 3

D. 4

----

59. Biohazardous materials most likely involving gloves and some sort of facial protection are used most likely when the biohazard level is below level:

A. 2

B. 3

C. 4

D. 5

----

60. According to the preceding passage, which of the following statements is not correct?

A. The parasite Plasmodium falciparum is classified in Biohazard Level 3.

B. Biohazard, Level 1 is extreme risk.

C. When dealing with biological hazards at Biohazard Level 4, the use of a positive pressure personnel suit, with a segregated air supply, is mandatory.

D. The letters "CDC" stand for "Centers for Disease Control."

CALIFORNIA POST EXAM GUIDE (PELLETB)

Instructions for Questions 61-105: In the following passages of text, certain words have been deleted and replaced by dashes (one dash for each letter of the word that has been deleted). Using the "contextual clues" in the paragraph, deduce the missing words and record your answers on the answer sheet, as instructed.

Passage 1:

New Year's Eve 61) _ _ celebrated all over 62) _ _ _ world. Major celebrations in the United States include the "ball-drop" in Times Square 63) _ _ _ the festivities on 64) _ _ _ Las Vegas Strip where many streets are closed off and large fireworks shows 65) _ _ _ held. Because of the large number 66) _ _ celebrants and the possibility of criminal activities, extra police 67) _ _ _ _ _ _ _ _ are assigned and special security measures 68) _ _ _ taken. Included 69) _ _ these measures is 70) _ _ increased effort to make 71) _ _ _ police force highly visible and thereby help prevent criminal 72) _ _ _ terrorist activities.

Passage 2:

Police Officers assigned to riot control must wear protective helmets 73) _ _ _ carry body shields. These items 74) _ _ _ designed to help protect officers while 75) _ _ _ _ are carrying out their duties. Because 76) _ _ the variety of other dangerous items 77) _ _ _ _ are often used 78) _ _ rioters, additional equipment 79) _ _ _ been developed. 80) _ _ _ example, to provide protection against airborne gas 81) _ _ _ biological agents, specialized gas masks and biological body suits 82) _ _ _ now available. 83) _ _ necessary, 84) _ _ _ _ _ _ officers may employ non-lethal crowd control items such 85) _ _ tear gas, Tasers, and 86) _ _ _ newly developed acoustic crowd control devices.

Passage 3:

Nelson Harkins 87) _ _ _ summoned to jury service 88) _ _ June 14, 2016. Following the directions on his juror notice, Nelson reported 89) _ _ 9:00 A.M. on that date to 360 Adams Street, Main Court Building. 90) _ _ _ central jury room was on the first 91) _ _ _ _ _ of the fifteen- story building. Nelson waited patiently 92) _ _ _ _ _ _ 11:15 A.M., when he heard his name called out on the loudspeaker. The person calling out 93) _ _ _ names identified herself

94) _ _ Senior Court Clerk Nancy Parsons. 95) _ _ _ instructed all fifty persons whose names she was calling to accompany 96) _ _ _ Court Officer waiting for them 97) _ _ the exit door.

Passage 4:

The desire 98) _ _ discover and share news has been documented since 99) _ _ _ beginning of recorded history. This desire seems to be ingrained 100) _ _ the human psyche and is thought to be as much 101) _ motivator as the desire for food and drink. 102) _ _ the speed of innovation 103) _ _ _ technological advancements has increased, so has the speed of sharing news. 104) _ _ _ _ the days of the first printing press to the spread of the internet, news dissemination has sped up dramatically. Today it is not unusual for a 105) _ _ _ _ item to spread worldwide in just a few minutes.

_____

Directions for Questions 106-110: In each of the following five questions, there is a number series. For each number series, you are to figure out the pattern in the series and determine what two numbers (represented by dashes) would be the last two numbers in the series.

-----

106)   90 60 86 56...82 52 ___ ___.
A) 85, 55   B) 77, 47   C) 50, 46   D) 78, 48

------

107)   70 73 76 79 82 85 __ __
A) 82, 86   B) 83, 87   C) 84, 86   D) 84, 88   E) 88, 91

------

108)   1 3 9 27 __ __
A) 81, 242   B) 80, 243   C) 79, 247   D) 81, 243

------

109)   30 30 34 34 38 38 42 42 __ __
A) 46, 46   B) 47, 47   C) 48, 48   D) 46, 47   E) 47, 46

------

110)   95 86 78 71 65 60 __ __

A) 56, 53   B) 56, 51   C) 58, 554   D) 55, 53

Directions: For questions 111-115, select the choice containing the word that does not belong in the group of the other three related words.

Question 111:

A. association

B. company

C. group

D. hermit

Question 112:

A. cafeteria

B. restaurant

C. coffee shop

D. chair

Question 113:

A. strap

B. cincture

C. bottle

D. sash

Question 114:

A. champion

B. winner

C. victor

D. candidate

Question 115:

A. fisherman

B. sportsman

C. huntsman

D. onlooker

Question 116

An illegal horde of cellphones was discovered in the suspect's warehouse: 87 Tamki brand flip phones, 135 Bambi brand juvenile cell phones, 117 Apple cell phones, 212 Humhu brand cell phones, and 172 Korlea brand cell phones. What is the brand name of the third biggest number of cell phones?

A. Humhu

B. Bambi

C. Korlea

D. Apple

Question 117

Your sergeant gives you five "Complaint Forms" with the following priority numbers:

3863   17648   0742   989   9244

He asks you to organize the forms in ascending priority.

According to the above, the third Complaint Form would be Complaint Form number:

A. 9244   C. 989

B. 0742   D. 3863

Question 118

Your sergeant gives you five "Requests for Investigation" forms submitted by residents in your precinct. The forms were submitted by the following five persons:

1) George Jenner, 2) Mike Weinfeld, 3) Dina Branson, 4) Ben Kerbin, 5) Conner, Brianna

He asks you to organize the forms in last name alphabetical order.

According to the above, the fourth "Request for Investigation" form is the one submitted by:

A. Weinfeld, Mike

B. Kerbin, Ben

C. Conner, Brianna

D. Branson, Dina

Directions for Questions 119-120: The following 2 questions are comprised of a series of sentences which are in scrambled order. Select the order of sentences (A, B, C, or D) which most correctly and logically places the sentences in a meaningful, logical, and effective order.

Question 119

1. Among these benefits are dental and optical benefits.

2. If you add to this amount, life insurance and other benefits, the total possible yearly benefit may exceed six or seven thousand dollars per family.

3. Court Assistants and Court Officers are represented by the New York State Court Officer's Association.

4. The combined amount of these two types of benefits may be two thousand dollars per year for each family member.

5. This association provides many quality benefits to its employees.

(A) 3-5-1-4-2

(B) 5-3-4-1-2

(C) 4-5-1-4-2

(D) 3-1-5-4-2

Question 120

1. They are restricted to these two outward aims because to test legal expertise would be unfair to the general public.

2. This aim is probably the most important and merit worthy aspect of civil service exams.

3. A third, invisible aim, is fairness.

4. They are designed to test general knowledge and aptitude only.

5. Some competitive civil service exams for positions in the court system do not include legal definitions.

(A) 3-1-5-4-2

(B) 5-4-1-3-2

(C) 4-5-1-4-2

(D) 5-1-3-4-2

PRACTICE TEST 2 ANSWERS

14

Instructions: For questions 1–15, select the choice with the correct spelling of the omitted word in the preceding sentence.

1. The lineup is scheduled for _____.

A. Tuesdey

B. Tusday

C. Tuesday

D. Teusday

-----

2. The _____ distributed a copy of the map to all the officers.

A. sargeant

B. sargent

C. sergant

D. sergeant

-----

3. The informant said that the suspect eats at the _____ on Friday nights.

A. restaurant

B. restorant

C. restarant

D. resterant

-----

4. She knew all the details because she was the _____ of the social club.

A. secratary

B. secretery

C. secritery

D. secretary

-----

5. In addition to being a mob boss, he was a _____ businessman.

A. successfull

B. sucsesful

C. successful

D. succesful

-----

6. The Captain said that this directive _____ the one issued last year.

A. supercedes

B. superceedes

C. superceeds

D. suppercedes

-----

7. Everyone was_____ by his quick confession.

A. supprised

B. surprised

C. suprised

D. surrprised

-----

8. He used the _____ cleaner cord to strangle him.

A. vaccuum

B. vacume

C. vaccume

D. vacuum

-----

9. The _____ agency reported the signs of child abuse.

A. wellfare

B. **welfare**

C. welfere

D. welfair

-----

10. Before he left, he conducted a _____ search.

A. thorough

B. thorugh

C. thorrow

D. thourogh

-----

11. The hostage taker announced that he wanted to make a _____ to the world.

A. speach

B. spiech

C. speech

D. speich

-----

12. The judge stated that the evidence was not _____ to the case.

A. relevant

B. relevent

C. rellevant

D. revelant

-----

13. He announced that he would not take his hat off in the courtroom because of _____

reasons.

A. religous

B. relligious

C. relligous

D. religious

-----

14. He said he would not pay the ticket on _____.

A. principal

B. principle

C. principel

D. princeple

-----

15. He was found guilty of _____ of heroin.

A. possesion

B. possession

C. posesion

D. posession

Instructions: For questions 16-30, choose the word that is closest in meaning to the underlined word in the sentence.

16. Although he stated that he wasn't fighting, the suspect looked underlined disheveled.

A. clean

B. neat

C. unwrinkled

D. ruffled (Ruffled is similar to disheveled, tousled, messed up.)

-----

17. He tried to extort a large sum of money from the bank.

A. offer

B. give

C. coerce (Coerce is similar to extort, extract, wrench.)

D. surrender

-----

18. The main reason why he fell for the scam was that he was young and impetuous.

A. cautious

B. impulsive (Impulsive is similar to hast, hurried, precipitant.)

C. calm

D. considerate

-----

19. Both he and his girlfriend had an irrational fear of riding in a car.

A. responsible

B. logical

C. sensible

D. unreasonable (Unreasonable is similar to nonsensical, reasonless, illogical.)

-----

20. She had no recollection of the car entering the danger zone.

A. vagueness

B. reason

C. memory (Memory is similar to recollection, recall, knowledge.)

D. purpose

-----

21. The handle of the screwdriver was protruding from the car's side door.

A. shrinking

B. extending (Extending is similar to protruding, extruding, butting out.)

C. contracting

D. depressing

-----

22. He saw the <u>silhouette</u> of the suspect in front of the partition.

A. brightness

B. contour (Contour is similar to silhouette, shape, form.)

C. light

D. brilliance

-----

23. He used the hose to <u>siphon</u> gas from the gas tank.

A. drain (Drain is similar to pump, funnel, extract.)

B. restore

C. return

D. restitute

-----

24. <u>Restitution</u> is often ordered in family court cases.

A. reimbursement (Reimbursement is similar to restitution, indemnity, indemnification.)

B. dissatisfaction

C. imprisonment

C. parole

-----

25. The attorney made two motions to <u>suppress</u> the introduction of the evidence.

A. allow

B. permit

C. sanction

D. repress (Repress is similar to suppress, muzzle, withhold.)

-----

26. His <u>adversary</u> was wearing a red business suit.

A. welcoming

B. hospitable

C. non-antagonistic

D. opponent (Opponent is similar to adversary, rival, antagonist.)

-----

27. Because of a lack of evidence, the allegation was not proven.

A. denial

B. accusation (Accusation is similar to allegation, contention, charge.)

C. disclaim

D. defense

-----

28. The <u>contusion</u> was on his forehead.

A. cure

B. healer

C. bruise (Bruise is similar to contusion, injury, swelling.)

D. treatment

-----

29. His statement was <u>corroborated</u> by two witnesses.

A. contradicted

B. substantiated (Substantiated is similar to corroborated, confirmed, supported.)

C. denied

D. disclaimed

-----

30. He was <u>detained</u> for a few hours.

A. confined (Confined is similar to detained, restrained, constrained.)

B. liberated

C. released

D. free

Instructions: For the following questions 15 questions, (Questions 31-45), decide which sentence is most clearly written.

Choose "A" if sentence "a" is clearer than sentence "b".
Choose "B" if sentence "b" is clearer than sentence "a".

Question 31:

a. The informant was seated at the table, he was very helpful.

b. The very helpful informant was seated at the table.

Answer 31: B ("a" is a run-on sentence.)

Question 32:

a. The victim pointed to the student who looked like the attacker in the class picture.

b. The victim pointed to the student in the class picture who looked like the attacker.

Answer 32: B ("b" is smoother and does not have the modification error that "a" has.)

Question 33:

a. The officer instructed the driver to take his driver's license out of his wallet and place it on the seat.

b. The officer instructed the driver to take his driver's license out of his wallet and place the license on the seat.

Answer 33: B ("a" has a reference error. It does not state clearly what the driver should place on the seat.)

Question 34:

a. The squad room is very tight, but they use it anyway.

b. The squad room is very tight, but the officers use it anyway.

Answer 34: B ("a" is confusing because it doesn't make clear who "they" are.)

Question 35:

a. The officer spotted the gold man's watch that was reported stolen.

b. The officer spotted the man's gold watch that was reported stolen.

Answer 35: B ("a" has a modification error. The correct version of "gold man's watch" is "man's gold watch".)

Question 36:

a. The volunteers took the cookies to the homeless shelter, where they were very much welcomed.

b. The volunteers took the cookies to the homeless shelter. Very much welcomed.

Answer 36: A ('b" has the sentence fragment, "Very much welcomed." The fragment contains the verb "welcomed", but it does not state what was welcomed.)

Question 37:

a. The witness threw out the toy, which was a mistake.

b. The witness made the mistake of throwing out the toy.

Answer 37: B ("a" contains a reference error. "Which was a mistake" does not make clear what was a mistake: the witness throwing out the toy OR the toy itself?)

Question 38:

a. The boxes were scattered in the parking lot. The tools were piled in front of the entrance.

b. The boxes were scattered in the parking lot, the tools were piled in front of the entrance.

Answer 13: A ("b" is a run-on sentence.)

Question 39:

a. Because of the "certain look," the gang members realized he had figured out their scheme.

b. Because of the "certain look" from the officer, the gang members realized he had figured out their scheme.

Answer 39: B ("a" has a modification error. Sentence "a" is confusing as to who has that "certain look" - the gang members or the police officer?)

Question 40:

a. The officer picked up the silver dirty pin from the floor.

b. The officer picked up the dirty silver pin from the floor.

Answer 40: B ("a" has a misplaced modifier. A "dirty silver pin" is smoother and clearer than " silver dirty pin.")

Question 41:

a. Seeing the child running away from her attacker, the officer's heart skipped in joy.

b. The officer's heart skipped in joy. Seeing the child running away from her attacker.

Answer 41: A ("b" contains the sentence fragment, " Seeing the child running away from her attacker.")

Question 42:

a. Even the rookie officers volunteered for overtime duty.

b. The officers volunteered for overtime duty. Even the rookie officers.

Answer 42: A ("b" contains a sentence fragment, "Even the rookie officers.")

Question 43:

a. The store owner thanked the sergeant for finding his missing pepper spray.

b. The store owner thanked the sergeant for finding the store owner's missing pepper spray.

Answer43: B ("a" is confusing because it is not clear whose pepper spray is missing. The "his" in "his pepper spray" does not make it clear whose pepper spray it is.)

Question 44:

a. Aided by the rookies, the senior officer completed the report on time.

b. The senior officer completed the report on time. Aided by the rookies.

Answer 44: A ("b" contains the sentence fragment, " Aided by the rookies.")

Question 45:

a. The officer put the gun in a box and told the rookie to take it to the evidence room.

b. The officer put the gun in a box and told the rookie to take the box to the evidence room.

Answer 45: B ("a" has a reference error. It does not state clearly what the rookie should take to the evidence room.)

For questions 46-47, read the following passage and then answer the questions based solely on the information provided in the passage.

A Police Officer must inform a person that she arrests that the person has the right to remain silent and that anything the person says may be used against the person in a court of law. The arresting officer must also inform the person that the person has the right to speak with an attorney before speaking with the arresting officer and that the person has the right to have an attorney present during questioning, and that if the person cannot afford an attorney, one will be provided by the state.

46.Which of the following statements is correct according to the above paragraph?

A. If an attorney is not present, a Police Officer shall not make an arrest.

B. Statements made by an arrested person may not be used in a court of law.

C. If a person can afford an attorney, the state will provide one.

D. A person may demand that an attorney be present during questioning.

----

47. Which of the following statements is not correct according to the above paragraph?

A. If the person cannot afford an attorney, one will be provided by the state.

B. The person has the right to remain silent.

C. The person must also inform the arresting officer that the person has the right to speak with an attorney before speaking with the arresting officer. (This is not correct because "The **arresting officer** must inform....")

D. The person has the right to have an attorney present during questioning.

For questions 48-49, read the following passage and then answer the questions based solely on the information provided in the passage.

The Americans With Disabilities Act applies to all court buildings, whether they are state owned or owned by private owners. It requires the California Court System to make reasonable accommodations for people with disabilities. In structures completed before January 1, 1994, reasonable accommodations may be made by physical modification of existing structures to meet ADA guidelines or by establishing procedures to otherwise reasonably accommodate people with disabilities. For example, in structures built after January 1, 1994, an entrance ramp must be provided where the first-floor entrance is above street level. In structures built before January 1, 1994 an alternative entrance, such as a back entrance, may be used if it provides access to the building at ground level.

-----

48. According to the above paragraph:

A. All back entrances to buildings must be at ground level.

B. An entrance ramp must be provided in all court buildings built after January 1, 1994.

C. Some ADA requirements do not require physical modification of existing structures.

D. ADA rules apply to all government buildings.

----

49. Which of the following four statements is not correct according to the above passage?

A. The Americans With Disabilities Act applies to all court buildings.

B. In certain structures, reasonable accommodations may be made by physical modification of existing structures to meet ADA guidelines.

C. The Americans With Disabilities Act requires the California Court System to make reasonable accommodations for people with disabilities.

D. In structures built after January 1, 1994 an alternative entrance, such as a back entrance, may be used if it provides access to the building at ground level.

(In structures built before January 1, 1994.....)

For questions 50-51, read the following passage and then answer the questions based solely on the information provided in the passage.

Although almost all court buildings are air conditioned, in some buildings there are some rooms or areas where the air conditioning system might not always be sufficient. This situation can occur because the power of the air conditioning system might not be adequate for the area, or because the system might need repair. If the temperature in a room rises above 84 degrees, then the employees must be relocated to another room. If there are no areas in the building where the temperature is below 84 degrees, then the employees shall be released with pay for the day. The release of the employees and the resulting suspension of court activity in the building must be prior approved by the head of Facilities, Brian Jenkins. In his absence, Vance Johnson of personnel relations may provide the same approval.

-----

50. According to the above passage, which of the following statements is not correct?

A. Employees working in a room must be relocated if the temperature rises above 84 degrees in the room.

B. If the temperature rises above 84 degrees in all the rooms of a court building, only Vance Johnson may approve the release of employees and suspension of court activity.

C. If employees are relocated to a different room, the temperature in the room to which they are relocated may not be more than 83 degrees.

D. Employees properly released due to excessive temperature do not lose any pay due to the release.

51. According to the preceding paragraph, which of the following statements is correct?

If the temperature in a room rises above 84 degrees, Vance Johnson, head of Facilities.

A. The temperature in a room may never rise above 84 degrees.

B. Vance Johnson is the head of Facilities.

C. Brian Jenkins works in personnel relations.

D. Not all court buildings are air-conditioned.

(Although **almost** all court buildings are air conditioned....)

For questions 52-53, read the following passage and then answer the questions based solely on the information provided in the passage.

Probationary Trainees receive approximately 16 weeks of training at the Probationary Trainees Academy, located at 87 Windham Place. The majority of the training is done in a classroom setting. In the classroom setting trainees receive instruction in such matters as public relations, criminal statutes, court procedures, first aid and crowd control. Training and qualification in the Glock semi-automatic are done at the firing range located at 12 Leonard Street. Following the academy training, Probationary Trainees are assigned to a specific town where they are further trained in the security and clerical procedures of that town. Although Probationary Trainees are primarily responsible for security, knowledge of clerical procedures helps them to better serve the public.

52. According to the above passage, which of the following statements is correct?

A. Training in the Glock semi-automatic is sometimes done at 87 Windham Street.

B. Probationary Trainees are primarily responsible for clerical procedures.

C. The Probationary Trainees Academy lasts approximately 4 weeks.

D. Security is the main responsibility of Probationary Trainees.

----

53. According to the above passage, which of the following statements is not correct?

A. Prior to attending the academy, a Probationary Trainee is assigned to a specific town.

(Trainees are assigned to a town after the training.)

B. The firing range is located at 12 Leonard Street.

C. The Probationary Trainees Academy is located at 87 Windham Place.

D. At the town of assignment, Probationary Trainees are further trained in clerical procedures.

For questions 54-55, read the following passage and then answer the questions based solely on the information provided in the passage.

In certain areas, Landlord and Tenant cases initiated by landlords are separated into two general categories, Non-Payments and Holdovers. Non-Payments seek an order of the court for the tenant to pay the owed rent or be evicted from the premises. Holdovers seek an order requiring the tenant to move and also the return of the premises to the landlord. The court fee for filing a Non-Payment or Holdover is $45.00 per case. This is paid to the cashier upon the issuance of an L&T number and must be in cash, certified check or money order made payable to the County Court. The fee for certification of court documents is $6.00. The transcript of judgment fee is $15.00.

-----

54. Which of the following statement is correct according to the above passage?

A. Holdovers seek an order requiring the tenant to pay the owed rent or be evicted from the premises.

B. Non-Payment proceedings are more numerous than Holdover proceedings.

C. The $45.00 filing fee may be paid by check made payable to the County Court.

D. Non-Payment proceedings seek the eviction of the tenant if the owed rent is not paid.

----

55. According to the above passage, which of the following statements is not correct?

A. The fee for certification of court documents is $6.00.

B. Non-Payments seek an order requiring the tenant to move and the return of the premises to the landlord

(**Holdovers** seek an order requiring the tenant to move and the return of the premises to the landlord)

C. The transcript of judgment fee is $15.00.

D. In some areas, Landlord and Tenant cases initiated by landlords are separated into two general categories, Non-Payments and Holdovers.

For questions 56-60, read the following passage and then answer the questions based solely on the information provided in the passage.

Biohazard Levels

The United States Centers for Disease Control and Prevention (CDC) categorizes various diseases in levels of biohazard, Level 1 being minimum risk and Level 4 being extreme risk.

Biohazard Level 1:

Bacteria and viruses including Bacillus subtilis, canine hepatitis, Escherichia coli, varicella (chicken pox), as well as some cell cultures and non-infectious bacteria. At this level precautions against the biohazardous materials in question are minimal, most likely involving gloves and some sort of facial protection.

Biohazard Level 2:

Bacteria and viruses that cause only mild disease to humans, or are difficult to contract via aerosol in a lab setting, such as hepatitis A, B, and C, influenza A, Lyme disease, salmonella, mumps, measles, scrapie, dengue fever.

Biohazard Level 3:

Bacteria and viruses that can cause severe to fatal disease in humans, but for which vaccines or other treatments exist, such as anthrax, West Nile virus, Venezuelan equine encephalitis, SARS virus, tuberculosis, typhus, Rift Valley fever, HIV, Rocky Mountain spotted fever, yellow fever, and malaria. Among parasites Plasmodium falciparum, which causes Malaria, and Trypanosoma cruzi, which causes trypanosomiasis, also come under this level.

Biohazard Level 4:

Viruses and bacteria that cause severe to fatal disease in humans, and for which vaccines or other treatments are not available, such as Bolivian and Argentine hemorrhagic fevers, Marburg virus, Ebola virus, hantaviruses, Lassa fever virus, Crimean–Congo hemorrhagic fever, and other hemorrhagic diseases. Variola virus (smallpox) is an agent that is worked with at BSL-4 despite the existence of a vaccine. When dealing with biological hazards at this level the use of a positive pressure personnel suit, with a segregated air supply, is mandatory.*

-----

56. According to the preceding "Biohazard Levels" passage, the highest and most dangerous biohazard risk is designated as:

A. Biohazard Level 1

B. Biohazard Level 2

C. Biohazard Level 3

D. Biohazard Level 4

(THIS IS THE CORRECT ANSWER. "The United States Centers for Disease Control and Prevention (CDC) categorizes various diseases in levels of biohazard, Level 1 being minimum risk and Level 4 being extreme risk.")

57. A "positive pressure personnel suit" must be used when dealing with Biohazard Level(s):

A. Biohazard Level 1 only.

B. Biohazard Levels 1 and 2 only.

C. Biohazard Level 1, 2, 3 and 4.

D. Biohazard Level 4.

(THIS IS THE CORRECT ANSWER. "Biohazard Level 4...When dealing with biological hazards at this level the use of a positive pressure personnel suit, with a segregated air supply, is mandatory.")

----

58. The parasite Plasmodium falciparum, which causes Malaria Malria, comes under Biohazard Level:

A. 1

B. 2

C. 3

(THIS IS THE CORRECT ANSWER. "Biohazard Level 3...Among parasites Plasmodium falciparum, which causes Malaria, and Trypanosoma cruzi, which causes trypanosomiasis, also come under this level.")

D. 4

----

59. Biohazardous materials most likely involving gloves and some sort of facial protection are used most likely when the biohazard level is below level:

A. 2

(THIS IS THE ANSWER. "Biohazard Level 1...At this level precautions against the biohazardous materials in question are minimal, most likely involving gloves and some sort of facial protection.")

B. 3

C. 4

D. 5

----

60. According to the preceding passage, which of the following statements is not correct?

A. The parasite Plasmodium falciparum is classified in Biohazard Level 3.

B. Biohazard, Level 1 is extreme risk.

(Level 1 is minimum risk.)

C. When dealing with biological hazards at Biohazard Level 4, the use of a positive pressure personnel suit, with a segregated air supply, is mandatory.

D. The letters "CDC" stand for "Centers for Disease Control."

CALIFORNIA POST EXAM GUIDE (PELLETB)

Instructions for Questions 61-105: In the following passages of text, certain words have been deleted and replaced by dashes (one dash for each letter of the word that has been deleted). Using the "contextual clues" in the paragraph, deduce the missing words and record your answers on the answer sheet, as instructed.

Passage 1:

New Year's Eve 61) _ _ celebrated all over 62) _ _ _ world. Major celebrations in the United States include the "ball-drop" in Times Square 63) _ _ _ the festivities on 64) _ _ _ Las Vegas Strip where many streets are closed off and large fireworks shows 65) _ _ _ held. Because of the large number 66) _ _ celebrants and the possibility of criminal activities, extra police 67) _ _ _ _ _ _ _ _ are assigned and special security measures 68) _ _ _ taken. Included 69) _ _ these measures is 70) _ _ increased effort to make 71) _ _ _ police force highly visible and thereby help prevent criminal 72) _ _ _ terrorist activities.

Passage 2:

Police Officers assigned to riot control must wear protective helmets 73) _ _ _ carry body shields. These items 74) _ _ _ designed to help protect officers while 75) _ _ _ _ are carrying out their duties. Because 76) _ _ the variety of other dangerous items 77) _ _ _ _ are often used 78) _ _ rioters, additional equipment 79) _ _ _ been developed. 80) _ _ _ example, to provide protection against airborne gas 81) _ _ _ biological agents, specialized gas masks and biological body suits 82) _ _ _ now available. 83) _ _ necessary, 84) _ _ _ _ _ _ officers may employ non-lethal crowd control items such 85) _ _ tear gas, Tasers, and 86) _ _ _ newly developed acoustic crowd control devices.

Passage 3:

Nelson Harkins 87) _ _ _ summoned to jury service 88) _ _ June 14, 2016. Following the directions on his juror notice, Nelson reported 89) _ _ 9:00 A.M. on that date to 360 Adams Street, Main Court Building. 90) _ _ _ central jury room was on the first 91) _ _ _ _ _ of the fifteen- story building. Nelson waited patiently 92) _ _ _ _ _ _ 11:15 A.M., when he heard his name called out on the loudspeaker. The person calling out 93) _ _ _ names identified herself

94) _ _ Senior Court Clerk Nancy Parsons. 95) _ _ _ instructed all fifty persons whose names she was calling to accompany 96) _ _ _ Court Officer waiting for them 97) _ _ the exit door.

Passage 4:

The desire 98) _ _ discover and share news has been documented since 99) _ _ _ beginning of recorded history. This desire seems to be ingrained 100) _ _ the human psyche and is thought to be as much 101) _ motivator as the desire for food and drink. 102) _ _ the speed of innovation 103) _ _ _ technological advancements have increased, so has the speed of sharing news. 104) _ _ _ _ the days of the first printing press to the spread of the internet, news dissemination has sped up dramatically. Today it is not unusual for a 105) _ _ _ _ item to spread worldwide in just a few minutes.

Answer for Questions 61-105:

61. is	76. of	91. floor
62. the	77. that	92. until
63. and	78. by	93. the
64. the	79. has	94. as
65. are	80. for	95. she
66. of	81. and	96. the
67. officers	82. are	97. by, at
68. are	83. if	98. to
69. in	84. police	99. the
70. an	85. as	100. in
71. the	86. the	101. a
72. and	87. was	102. as
73. and	88. on	103. and
74. are	89. at	104. from
75. they	90. the	105. news

Directions for Questions 106-110: In each of the following five questions, there is a number series. For each number series, you are to figure out the pattern in the series and determine what two numbers (represented by dashes) would be the last two numbers in the series.

-----

106)   90 60 86 56...82 52 ___ ___.

A) 85, 55   B) 77, 47   C) 50, 46   D) 78, 48

Answer 106: D) 78, 48

Pattern is two **DOUBLE** numbers (90 and 60) **ALTERNATING** and **DECREASING** by 4 each time.

----

107)   70 73 76 79 82 85 __ __

A) 82, 86   B) 83, 87   C) 84, 86   D) 84, 88   E) 88, 91

Answer 107: E (88, 91)

Pattern is the number 70 **INCREASING** by 3 each time the pattern is repeated.

----

108)   1 3 9 27 __ __

A) 81, 242   B) 80, 243   C) 79, 247   D) 81, 243

Answer 108: D (81, 243)

Pattern is 1 **MULTIPLIED** by 3 each time the pattern is repeated (1 X 3 = 3, 3 X 3 = 9, 9 X 3 = 27, 27 X 3 = 81, 81 X 3 = 243).

----

109)   30 30 34 34 38 38 42 42 __ __

A) 46, 46   B) 47, 47   C) 48, 48   D) 46, 47   E) 47, 46

Answer 109: A (46, 46)

The pattern is the number 30 **REPEATED** once and then **INCREASED** by 4 each time the pattern is repeated (30, Repeat 30, 30 + 4 = 34, Repeat 34, 34 + 4 = 38, Repeat 38, 38 + 4 = 42, Repeat 42, 42 + 4 = 46, Repeat 46).

----

110)   95 86 78 71 65 60 __ __

A) 56, 53   B) 56, 51   C) 58, 554   D) 55, 53

Answer 110: A (56, 53)

The pattern is the number 95 DECREASING by a DECREASING number each time the pattern is repeated (95 - 9 = 86, 86 - 8 = 78, 78 - 7 = 71, 71 - 6 = 65, 65 - 5 = 60, 60 - 4 = 56, 56 - 3 = 53).

Directions: For questions 111-115, select the choice containing the word that does not belong in the group of the other three related words.

Question 111:

A. association

B. company

C. group

D. hermit (The other 3 words refer to groups of people. Hermit is one individual.)

Question 112:

A. cafeteria

B. restaurant

C. coffee shop

D. chair (The other 3 words are places, generally where people meet and eat. Chair is an object that can be found anywhere.)

Question 113:

A. strap

B. cincture

C. bottle (The other 3 words are items that are worn on the body. Bottle is a physical item that holds a liquid and may be placed on or near a variety of objects.)

D. sash

Question 114:

A. champion

B. winner

C. victor

D. candidate (The other 3 words refer to persons who are "number one." A candidate is simply one who participates.)

Question 115:

A. fisherman

B. sportsman

C. huntsman

D. onlooker (The other 3 words relate to people who actively hunt and fish. Onlooker is one who does not personally participate.)

Question 116

An illegal horde of cellphones was discovered in the suspect's warehouse: 87 Tamki brand flip phones, 135 Bambi brand juvenile cell phones, 117 Apple cell phones, 212 Humhu brand cell phones, and 172 Korlea brand cell phones. What is the brand name of the third biggest number of cell phones?

A. Humhu

B. Bambi

C. Korlea

D. Apple

(The order, according to the number of cell phones, is: 1) Tamki (87), 2) Apple (117), 3) Bambi (135), 4) Korlea (172), and 5) Humhu (212).)

Question 117

Your sergeant gives you five "Complaint Forms" with the following priority numbers:

3863   17648   0742   989   9244

He asks you to organize the forms in ascending priority.

According to the above, the third Complaint Form would be Complaint Form number:

A. 9244   C. 989

B. 0742   D. 3863

The Complaint Forms in Ascending Priority Number Order are as follows:

1) 0742

2) 989

3) 3863

4) 9244

5) 17648

The third complaint number on the list is 3863. Therefore, the correct answer is **D) 3863.**

Question 118

Your sergeant gives you five "Requests for Investigation" forms submitted by residents in your precinct. The forms were submitted by the following five persons:

1) George Jenner, 2) Mike Weinfeld, 3) Dina Branson, 4) Ben Kerbin, 5) Conner, Brianna

He asks you to organize the forms in last name alphabetical order.

According to the above, the fourth "Request for Investigation" form is the one submitted by:

A. Weinfeld, Mike

B. Kerbin, Ben

C. Conner, Brianna

D. Branson, Dina

Answer 118

The correct listing in last name alphabetical order is:

1) Branson, Dina

2) Conner, Brianna

3) Jenner, George

4) Kerbin, Ben

5) Weinfeld, Mike

The fourth name on the list is Kerbin, Ben, therefore the correct answer is **B. Kerbin, Ben**

Directions for Questions 119-120: The following 2 questions are comprised of a series of sentences which are in scrambled order. Select the order of sentences (A, B, C, or D) which most correctly and logically places the sentences in a meaningful, logical, and effective order.

Question 119

1. Among these benefits are dental and optical benefits.

2. If you add to this amount, life insurance and other benefits, the total possible yearly benefit may exceed six or seven thousand dollars per family.

3. Court Assistants and Court Officers are represented by the New York State Court Officer's Association.

4. The combined amount of these two types of benefits may be two thousand dollars per year for each family member.

5. This association provides many quality benefits to its employees.

(A) 3-5-1-4-2

(B) 5-3-4-1-2

(C) 4-5-1-4-2

(D) 3-1-5-4-2

Answer 119: (A) 3-5-1-4-2

(3) Court Assistants and Court Officers are represented by the New York State Court Officer's Association.

(5) This association provides many quality benefits to its employees.

(1) Among these benefits are dental and optical benefits.

(4) The combined amount of these two types of benefits may be two thousand dollars per year for each family member.

(2) If you add to this amount, life insurance and other benefits, the total possible yearly benefit may exceed six or seven thousand dollars per family.

Question 120

1. They are restricted to these two outward aims because to test legal expertise would be unfair to the general public.

2. This aim is probably the most important and merit worthy aspect of civil service exams.

3. A third, invisible aim, is fairness.

4. They are designed to test general knowledge and aptitude only.

5. Some competitive civil service exams for positions in the court system do not include legal definitions.

(A) 3-1-5-4-2

(B) 5-4-1-3-2

(C) 4-5-1-4-2

(D) 5-1-3-4-2

Answer 120: (B) 5-4-1-3-2

(5) Open competitive civil service exams for positions in the court system do not include legal definitions.

(4) They are designed to test general knowledge and aptitude only.

(1) They are restricted to these two outward aims because to test legal expertise would be unfair to the general public.

(3) A third, invisible aim, therefore, is fairness.

(2) This aim is probably the most important and merit worthy aspect of civil service exams.

PRACTICE TEST 3 QUESTIONS

15

Instructions: For questions 1–15, select the choice with the correct spelling of the omitted word in the preceding sentence.

1. The suspect stated that he attacked the victim because the victim _____ him.

A. embarased

B. embarrased

C. embaressed

D. embarrassed

-----

2. He _____ made the statue topple and break.

A. accidentaly

B. accidentally

C. acidentaly

D. accidantaly

-----

3. Her goal is hard to _____.

A. acheive

B. achive

C. acheve

D. achieve

-----

4. When did he _____ all of his wealth?

A. acquire

B. adquire

C. acquirre

D. aquire

-----

5. The jury _____ him because they were convinced of his innocence.

A. ackuitted

B. acquitted

C. aquitted

D. akuitted

-----

6. The witness said that he always wanted to win the _____.

A. arguement

B. argument

C. arguemment

D. argumment

-----

7. Because of the officer's diligence, the _____ attempt failed.

A. asasination

B. assassination

C. asassination

D. assasination

-----

8. The psychiatrist testified that the defendant had pent-up _____.

A. aggresion

B. agression

C. agresion

D. aggression

-----

9. He was required to pay the dues _____.

A. anually

B. anualy

C. annualy

D. annually

-----

10. The suspect is a _____ of the business owner.

A. colleague

B. colegue

C. collegue

D. collaegue

-----

11. It was Officer Spencer who _____ the burglar.

A. cauhgt

B. caugt

C. caught

D. caute

-----

12. She accused him of abandonment and _____.

A. adultery

B. adultary

C. adeltury

D. addultery

-----

13. The restaurant owner said he had done everything possible to _____ the customer.

A. acomodate

B. acommodate

C. accomodate

D. accommodate

-----

14. The _____ between them had been going on for two years.

A. contraversy

B. controversy

C. kontroversy

D. contravarsy

-----

15. He realized that his actions had placed him in a serious _____.

A. dilema

B. dealemma

C. delema

D. dilemma

Instructions: For questions 16-30, choose the word that is closest in meaning to the underlined word in the sentence.

16. He complained that because of his short stature, he was the subject of <u>derision</u> by all the other classmates.

A. mockery

B. admiration

C. approval

D. praise

-----

17. After considering all the facts, the jury concluded that the <u>negligent</u> party was the driver of the Toyota.

A. attentive

B. thoughtful

C. native

D. careless

-----

18. At the scene of the accident, he discovered a <u>prodigious</u> amount of evidence.

A. insignificant

B. unremarkable

C. tremendous

D. small

-----

19. As soon as he stopped attending their meetings, he <u>repudiated</u> the gang and all its rules.

A. disavowed

B. accepted

C. enforced

D. approved

-----

20. Because he transferred the funds under a false name, he was charged with <u>embezzlement</u>.

A. negligence

B. incompetence

C. blunder

D. larceny

-----

21. The use of drugs was <u>prevalent</u> in the 9th District.

A. common

B. exceptional

C. scarce

D. limited

-----

22. The motive remained an <u>enigma</u> until the first day of trial.

A. certainty

B. mystery

C. clearness

D. certainty

-----

23. Based on the witness accounts, the motive was <u>unequivocal</u>.

A. ambiguous

B. apparent

C. unclear

D. vague

-----

24. Fueled by his drug abuse, his tears were <u>incessant</u>.

A. intermittent

B. unending

C. interrupted

D. broken

-----

25. The possibility of being discovered and punished was the major <u>deterrent</u> to committing the burglary.

A. assistance

B. encouragement

C. disincentive

D. incentive

26. Although the charge was substantiated, his answers were <u>flippant</u>.

A. serious

B. courteous

C. respectful

D. frivolous

-----

27. The drugs were being processed by Elmore Labs and its <u>subsidiary</u>.

A. opponent

B. headquarters

C. branch

D. neighbor

-----

28. He gained the trust of the charitable contributors by appearing to be a <u>benevolent</u> person.

A. cruel

B. caring

C. miserly

D. malevolent

-----

29. When we extracted him from the rubble, his complexion was <u>pallid</u>.

A. healthy

B. hearty

C. strong

D. pale

-----

30. The heavy and bulky climbing equipment was a <u>hindrance</u> to the special officer.

A. aid

B. handicap

C. assistance

D. benefit

Instructions: For the following questions 15 questions, (Questions 31-45), decide which sentence is most clearly written.

Choose "A" if sentence "a" is clearer than sentence "b".
Choose "B" if sentence "b" is clearer than sentence "a".

Question 31:

a. Seeing the robber head for the back door, adrenalin started flowing.

b. When he spotted the robber heading for the back door, the officer's adrenalin started flowing.

Question 32:

a. Even the spectators across the street felt the blast of the explosion.

b. The spectators felt the blast of the explosion. Even the ones across the street.

Question 33:

a. The captain commended the officer for finding his missing hat.

b. The captain commended the officer for finding the captain's missing hat.

Question 34:

a. The officer and the witness is on route to the court hearing.

b. The officer and the witness are on route to the court hearing.

Question 35:

a. Because he used the van, the officer was able to transport the riot gear.

b. The officer was able to transport the riot gear. Because he used the van.

Question 36:

a. The fireworks show was on a small island in the middle of the wide river. The spectators were on the east side of the river.

b. The fireworks show was on a small island in the middle of the wide river, the spectators were on the east side of the river.

Question 37:

a. The mentally incompetent suspect confessed that he wanted everything he saw advertised, even though he often didn't understand what purpose they served.

b. The mentally incompetent suspect confessed that he wanted everything he saw advertised, even though he often didn't understand what purpose the items served.

Question 38:

a. While breathing through their gas mask filters, the officers marched in a straight line.

b. The officers marched in a straight line. Breathing through their gas mask filters.

Question 39:

a. After the officer and the victim spoke, he had a good idea.

b. After the officer spoke with the victim, the officer had a good idea.

Question 40:

a. The squad car made a rickety noise. It needed a tune-up.

b. The squad car made a rickety noise, it needed a tune-up.

Question 41:

a. Blowing out black fumes, Officer Follins called in a repair request.

b. Because the car was blowing out black fumes, Officer Follins called in a repair request.

Question 42:

a. The items on the list of chores were long and difficult, especially the last four items.

b. The items on the list of chores were long and difficult. Especially the last four items.

Question 43:

a. Because the purple man's vase was broken in only two pieces, he had it glued back together.

b. Because the man's purple vase was broken in only two pieces, he had it glued back together.

Question 44:

a. He ate the spaghetti and drank red wine. Waiting for his employee to pick him up.

b. While waiting for his employee to pick him up, he ate spaghetti and drank red wine.

Question 45:

a. After placing the bracelet in a red pouch, she took it to her apartment.

b. After placing the bracelet in a red pouch, she took the pouch to her apartment.

For questions 46-47, read the following passage and then answer the questions based solely on the information provided in the passage.

"Terrorism" comes from the French word terrorisme, and originally referred specifically to state terrorism as practiced by the French government during the 1793–1794 Reign of Terror. The French word terrorisme in turn derives from the Latin verb terrere (e, terreo) meaning "to frighten". The Jacobins, coming to power in France in 1792, are said to have initiated the Reign of Terror (French: La Terreur). After the Jacobins lost power, the word "terrorist" became a term of abuse.

Although "terrorism" originally referred to acts committed by a government, currently it usually refers to the killing of innocent people for political purposes in such a way as to create a spectacle. This meaning can be traced back to Sergey Nechayev, who described himself as a "terrorist". Nechayev founded the Russian terrorist group "People's Retribution" in 1869.*

-----

46. Based on the preceding passage, which of the following statements is correct?

A. The word "terrorism" has always meant the same thing.

B. The Latin verb "terrere" derives from the French verb "terrorisme."

C. The Jacobins came to power in France in 1729.

D. The word "terrorist" became a term of abuse after the Jacobins lost power.

----

47. Based on the preceding passage, which of the following statements is not correct?

A. Sergey Nechayev, described himself as a "terrorist".

B. The Jacobins are said to have initiated the Reign of Terror.

C. "Terrorism" originally referred to acts committed by mobs of people.

D. "Terrorism" comes from the French word terrorisme.

For questions 48-49, read the following passage and then answer the questions based solely on the information provided in the passage.

The lack of consensus as to what a terrorist is can affect policies designed to deal with terrorists. Some view them as soldiers that can be held at the end of a war and are entitled to various privileges spelled out in the Geneva Conventions. Others view them as criminals that should be tried in civil courts. Still others will argue that terrorists are best treated as a category to themselves and need policies tailored to them.

In November 2004, a Secretary-General of the United Nations report described terrorism as any act "intended to cause death or serious bodily harm to civilians or non-combatants with the purpose of intimidating a population or compelling a government or an international organization to do or abstain from doing any act".*

-----

48. According to the preceding passage, some people define terrorists as one of the following, except:

A. people in a category to themselves.

B. criminals

C. soldiers

D. politicians

----

49. According to the preceding passage, which of the following statements is not correct?

A. The title of the official of the United Nations mentioned in the passage is "Secretary-Genial."

B. There is a lack of consensus as to what a terrorist is.

C. Some people view terrorists as criminals.

D. The terrorism report by the Secretary-General of the United Nations was dated November 2004.

For questions 50-51, read the following passage and then answer the questions based solely on the information provided in the passage.

The Glock pistol, sometimes referred to by the manufacturer as a Glock "Safe Action" pistol and colloquially as a Glock, is a series of polymer-framed, short recoil-operated, locked-breech semi-automatic pistols designed and produced by Glock Ges.m.b.H., located in Deutsch-Wagram, Austria. It entered Austrian military and police service by 1982 after it was the top performer on an exhaustive series of reliability and safety tests.

Despite initial resistance from the market to accept a "plastic gun" due to durability and reliability concerns, and fears, (subsequently shown to be unfounded), that the pistol would be "invisible" to metal detectors in airports, Glock pistols have become the company's most profitable line of products, commanding 65% of the market share of handguns for United States law enforcement agencies, as well as supplying numerous national armed forces, security agencies, and police forces in at least 48 countries. Glocks are also popular firearms among civilians for recreational and competition shooting, home and self-defense, and concealed carry or open carry.*

-----

50. Which of the following statements is not correct, according to the preceding paragraph?

A. Glock pistols have become the company's most profitable line of products.

B. Glock pistols have a 56% share of the market share of handguns for United States law enforcement agencies.

C. The Glock pistol is referred to colloquially as a Glock,

D. Glocks are also popular firearms among civilians for recreational and competition shooting.

----

51. According to the preceding passage, which of the following statements is not correct?

A. The Glock is referred to by the manufacturer as a Glock "Safe Action" pistol.

B. Metal pistols have become the company's most profitable line of products.

C. Glocks are used by police forces in 48 countries.

D. The Glock entered Austrian military and police service by 1982.

For questions 52-55, read the following passage and then answer the questions based solely on the information provided in the passage.

Concealed carry or carrying a concealed weapon (CCW), is the practice of carrying a weapon (such as a handgun) in public in a concealed manner, either on one's person or in close proximity. Not all weapons that fall under CCW laws are lethal. For example, in Florida, carrying pepper spray in more than a specified volume (2 oz.) of chemical requires a CCW permit, whereas anyone may legally carry a smaller, so-called, "self-defense chemical spray" device hidden on their person without a CCW permit.

There is no federal statutory law concerning the issuance of concealed-carry permits. All fifty states have passed laws allowing qualified individuals to carry certain concealed firearms in public, either without a permit or after obtaining a permit from a designated government authority at the state and/or local level. Vermont does not have such a statute but permits both open and concealed carry based on a court decision of long standing. Illinois had been the last state without such a provision – but its long-standing ban on concealed weapons was overturned in a federal appeals court, on Constitutional grounds. Illinois was ordered by the court to draft a concealed carry law by July 9, 2013 (including a 30-day extension) at which time the Illinois legislature, overriding the amendatory veto of the governor, approved legislation to permit and regulate concealed carry to begin by January 2014.*

-----

52. According to the above passage, which of the following statements is not correct?

A. All fifty states have passed laws allowing qualified individuals to carry certain concealed firearms in public.

B In Florida, carrying pepper spray in more than a specified volume (2 oz.) of chemical requires a CCW permit.

C. All weapons that fall under CCW laws are lethal.

D. There is no federal statutory law concerning the issuance of concealed-carry permits.

----

53. According to the preceding passage, which of the following statements is not correct?

A. For example, in Florida, carrying pepper spray in more than a specified volume (2 oz.) of chemical requires a CCW permit,

B. Concealed carry or carrying a concealed weapon (CCW), is the practice of carrying a weapon (such as a handgun) in public in a concealed manner.

C. "In a public manner" is described as either on one's person or in close proximity.

D. There are no state statutory laws concerning the issuance of concealed-carry permits.

----

54. According to the preceding passage, "In a concealed manner" is defined as:

A. the practice of carrying a weapon in public in a concealed manner on one's person only.

B. the practice of carrying a weapon in public in a concealed manner in close proximity to the person only.

C. the practice of owning a weapon illegally.

D. the practice of carrying a weapon in public in a concealed manner, either on one's person or in close proximity.

----

55. According to the above passage, which of the following is a logical conclusion?

A. Puerto Rico does not have a law regarding concealed-carry permits.

B. All fifty states do not allow concealed weapons.

C. Vermont allows the carrying of concealed weapons.

D. The CCW is a private lobby group.

For questions 56-60, read the following passage and then answer the questions based solely on the information provided in the passage.

The California system has been the origin of many trends in prison conditions within the United States as a whole. The state's large and diverse population, large size, large urban areas, high rates of violent crime, criminal street gangs, tough sentencing laws and its status as an entry point to the U.S. for both immigrants and drugs has given California a large and complex prison environment. California prisons are overcrowded, with a number of facilities holding more than 200% of their design capacity.

The system, like the state as a whole, lacks a racial/ethnic majority among the population. Prisoner identification and affiliation is tied closely to race and region of the state, which has contributed to tension and violence. There has been a long running racial tension between African American and Southern Mexican American prison gangs and significant riots in California prisons where Mexican inmates and African Americans have targeted each other particularly, based on racial reasons. California is the birthplace of the United States' most powerful and well-known prison gangs, including the Aryan Brotherhood, Mexican Mafia, Nuestra Familia, and the Black Guerrilla Family. State efforts against these gangs made California a pioneer in the development of Security Housing Unit "supermax" control-unit facilities.

The overcrowded conditions and accusations of inadequate medical facilities and mistreatment have caused the federal courts to intervene in the system's operation since the 1990s, appointing special oversight and enforcing consent decrees over the system's medical system and the SHU units and capping populations at several facilities. As of 2007, by order of federal courts, the system's medical system is under federal receivership, and a federal court may impose a mandatory limit on the system's total inmate population.*

-----

56. According to the above passage:

A. The "Nusestra Familia" is a well-known prison gangs.

B. California prisons are not yet overcrowded.

C. Prisoner identification and affiliation is tied closely to race and region of the state.

D. The system's medical system has received a federal commendation.

----

57. The federal court has done each of the following, except:

A. intervening in the system's operation.

B. appointing special oversight.

C. enforcing consent decrees.

D. releasing some prisoners to reduce overcrowding.

----

58. California is the birthplace of the United States' of the following most powerful and well-known prison gangs, except:

A. Mexican Mafia

B. Aryan Brotherhood

C. Nuestra Famiglia.

D. Breaker Guerilla Family.

----

59. Which of the following factors contributing to California's large and complex prison environment is not mentioned in the preceding passage?

A. high rates of violent crime

B. large urban areas

C. conservative judges.

D. tough sentencing laws

----

60. According to the above passage:

A. Blacks make up the majority of the prison population.

B. Hispanics make up less than fifty percent of the prison population.

C. The prison system lacks a racial/ethnic majority among the population.

D. There is no tension between African American and Southern Mexican American prison gangs.

CALIFORNIA POST EXAM GUIDE (PELLETB)

Instructions for Questions 61-105: In the following passages of text, certain words have been deleted and replaced by dashes (one dash for each letter of the word that has been deleted). Using the "contextual clues" in the paragraph, deduce the missing words and record your answers on the answer sheet, as instructed.

Passage 1:

The handgun 61) _ _ generally considered 62) _ _ _ smallest of all firearms. Single-shot pistols were used in historical times. However, today the 63) _ _ _ main categories of handguns 64) _ _ _ revolvers and semi-automatic pistols. Revolvers shoot single rounds drawn from one of the "charge holes" in a revolving cylinder. Semi-automatics draw their rounds 65) _ _ _ _ a magazine and can fire more than 66) _ _ _ round at a time.

Passage 2:

After arraignment and before entry of plea 67) _ _ guilty or commencement of trial, the court may upon motion of the people 68) _ _ defendant, or upon its own motion and consent of both the people and the defendant, order 69) _ _ ACD (ADJOURNMENT IN CONTEMPLATION OF DISMISSAL). 70) _ _ _ case is adjourned without 71) _ date. People may make an application 72) _ _ restore the case within 6 months. 73) _ _ that occurs, the court may restore it 74) _ _ _ proceed to trial. 75) _ _ the case is not restored, the accusatory instrument is deemed to have been dismissed in furtherance of justice at the end of the six-month period.

Passage 3:

Tardiness is the 76) _ _ _ _ _ _ _ _ of punctuality. To be punctual means to 77) _ _ on time, while tardiness means 78) _ _ _ habit of being late. In the United States, tardiness is frowned upon. In the workplace, 79) _ _ employee who is habitually tardy may 80) _ _ charged with misconduct 81) _ _ _ may be punished. 82) _ _ _ _ punishment may include demotion or termination of employment. However, not 83) _ _ _ cultures punish tardiness. 84) _ _ Africa, where a more relaxed lifestyle 85) _ _ preferred, tardiness is generally accepted as part of 86) _ _ _ lifestyle.

Passage 4:

When a criminal case 87) _ _ pending in 88) _ _ _ courts, the Police Officer who made the arrest 89) _ _ prohibited from discussing the case 90) _ _ _ _ any newspaper, magazine, TV reporters and all other media. Exceptions 91) _ _ this are 1) cases where a California court of competent jurisdiction formally orders the Police 92) _ _ _ _ _ _ _ to discuss one or more particulars of the case, 2) a California authorized Department orders such discussion, 3) the Police Officer 93) _ _ subpoenaed to testify by an authorized California State board 94) _ _ federal board.

Passage 5:

Police 95) _ _ _ _ _ _ _ _ Jack Ellis and Rhonda Cordan were 96) _ _ patrol on November 3, 2014 when at 7:15 p.m. 97) _ _ _ _ they witnessed a minor traffic accident (in front of 2455 Elmer Street, in Woodmere). Officer Ellis called 98) _ _ _ Police Dispatcher 99) _ _ 7:25 p.m. 100) _ _ _ reported that the two drivers 101) _ _ _ four passengers 102) (_ _ in each vehicle) did not sustain any personal injuries. 103) _ _ _ of the vehicles, the one driven 104) _ _ a male named Fred Ulmer, did have minor damage to the driver's side door, and the other vehicle, driven by a male named Oswald Trunger, had minor damage to 105) _ _ _ front bumper.

Directions for Questions 106-110: In each of the following five questions, there is a number series. For each number series, you are to figure out the pattern in the series and determine what two numbers (represented by dashes) would be the last two numbers in the series.

-----

106)　　　　53　30　51　28...49　26　___ ___.

A) 45, 22　　　　B) 47, 24　　　　C) 55, 32　　　　D) 45, 20

----

107)　　　　70　79　88　97　106　115　__　__

A) 122,131　　　　B) 124, 134　　　　C) 124, 135　　　　D) 124, 133

----

108)   2 6 18 54 __ __

A) 162, 486   B) 160, 484   C) 158, 488   D) 162, 484

----

109)   30 30 33 33 36 36 39 39 __ __

A) 46, 46   B) 42, 42   C) 48, 48   D) 46, 47

----

110)   93 84 76 69 63 58 __ __

A) 53, 51   B) 54, 51   C) 54, 52   D) 52, 53   E) 52, 51

Directions: For questions 111-115, select the choice containing the word that does not belong in the group of the other three related words.

Question 111:

A. feast

B. celebration

C. gala

D. funeral

Question 112:

A. thicket

B. forest

C. woodland

D. clearing

Question 113:

A. examination

B. inspection

C. instrument

D. probe

Question 114:

A. drink

B. libation

C. brew

D. steak

Question 115:

A. old

B. aged

C. mature

D. embryonic

Question 116

Four firearms were found at the suspect's house. One firearm was a 45 caliber semi-automatic pistol. Another was a 38-caliber mini gun. Another was a home-made 12-caliber one-shot firearm. The other was a 50-caliber military weapon. Which of the following is the third highest caliber weapon found?

A. the military weapon

B. the mini-gun

C. the homemade on-shot firearm

D. the semi-automatic pistol

Question 117

Your sergeant gives you five "Complaint Forms" with the following priority numbers:

9457   13647   0659   758   8793

He asks you to organize the forms in ascending priority.

According to the above, the third Complaint Form would be Complaint Form number:

A. 9457   C. 13647

B. 0758   D. 8793

Question 118

Your sergeant gives you five "Requests for Investigation" forms submitted by residents in your precinct. The forms were submitted by the following five persons:

1) James Vaccaro, 2) Carol Gomez, 3) William Jones, 4) Erika Whitfield, 5) Frances Diamond

He asks you to organize the forms in last name alphabetical order.

According to the above, the fourth "Request for Investigation" form is the one submitted by:

A. William, Jones

B. Vaccaro, James

C. Gomez, Carol

D. Whitfield, Erika

Directions for Questions 119-120: The following 2 questions are comprised of a series of sentences which are in scrambled order. Select the order of sentences (A, B, C, or D) which most correctly and logically places the sentences in a meaningful, logical, and effective order.

Question 119

1. Everyone is different, and there may be as many ways to study as there are people.

2. This does not mean, however, that all neural connections and all brains work alike.

3. Short sessions help the brain retain more, while studying over a period of time help to reinforce the neural connections in the brain.

4. Short study sessions over a long period of time are very helpful.

5. The manner and length of time that one practices answering questions can greatly affect the mark that one receives on an exam.

(A) 5-1-3-4-2

(B) 5-4-1-3-2

(C) 4-5-1-4-2

(D) 5-4-3-2-1

Question 120:

1. State permanent employees receive 20 days of paid vacation during their first year of service, in addition to 11 paid holidays.

2. The total of all these three types of benefit days is 54.

3. The State offers many types of benefits to its permanent employees.

4. They also accrue 13 days of paid annual sick leave.

5. In addition to pension benefits, it offers three types of paid days.

(A) 5-3-1-2-4   (C) 5-3-2-4-2

(B) 3-5-1-2-4   (D) 3-5-1-42

PRACTICE TEST 3 ANSWERS

16

Instructions: For questions 1–15, select the choice with the correct spelling of the omitted word in the preceding sentence.

1. The suspect stated that he attacked the victim because the victim _____ him.

A. embarased

B. embarrased

C. embaressed

D. embarrassed

-----

2. He _____ made the statue topple and break.

A. accidentaly

B. accidentally

C. acidentaly

D. accidantaly

-----

3. Her goal is hard to _____.

A. acheive

B. achive

C. acheve

D. achieve

-----

4. When did he _____ all of his wealth?

A. acquire

B. adquire

C. acquirre

D. aquire

-----

5. The jury _____ him because they were convinced of his innocence.

A. ackuitted

B. acquitted

C. aquitted

D. akuitted

-----

6. The witness said that he always wanted to win the _____.

A. arguement

B. argument

C. arguemment

D. argumment

-----

7. Because of the officer's diligence, the _____ attempt failed.

A. asasination

B. assassination

C. asassination

D. assasination

-----

8. The psychiatrist testified that the defendant had pent-up _____.

A. aggresion

B. agression

C. agresion

D. aggression

-----

9. He was required to pay the dues _____.

A. anually

B. anualy

C. annualy

D. annually

-----

10. The suspect is a _____ of the business owner.

A. colleague

B. colegue

C. collegue

D. collaegue

-----

11. It was Officer Spencer who _____ the burglar.

A. cauhgt

B. caugt

C. caught

D. caute

-----

12. She accused him of abandonment and _____.

A. adultery

B. adultary

C. adeltury

D. addultery

-----

13. The restaurant owner said he had done everything possible to _____ the customer.

A. acomodate

B. acommodate

C. accomodate

D. accommodate

-----

14. The _____ between them had been going on for two years.

A. contraversy

B. controversy

C. kontroversy

D. contravarsy

-----

15. He realized that his actions had placed him in a serious _____.

A. dilema

B. dealemma

C. delema

D. dilemma

CALIFORNIA POST EXAM GUIDE (PELLETB)

<u>Instructions</u>: **For questions 16-30, choose the word that is closest in meaning to the underlined word in the sentence.**

16. He complained that because of his short stature, he was the subject of <u>derision</u> by all the other classmates.

A. mockery (Mockery is similar to derision, ridicule, disparagement.)

B. admiration

C. approval

D. praise

-----

17. After considering all the facts, the jury concluded that the <u>negligent</u> party was the driver of the Toyota.

A. attentive

B. thoughtful

C. native

D. careless (Careless is similar to negligent, irresponsible, reckless.)

-----

18. At the scene of the accident, he discovered a <u>prodigious</u> amount of evidence.

A. insignificant

B. unremarkable

C. tremendous (Tremendous is similar to colossal, vast, massive.)

D. small

-----

19. As soon as he stopped attending their meetings, he <u>repudiated</u> the gang and all its rules.

A. disavowed (Disavowed is similar to abandoned, dismissed, disclaimed.)

B. accepted

C. enforced

D. approved

-----

20. Because he transferred the funds under a false name, he was charged with <u>embezzlement</u>.

A. negligence

B. incompetence

C. blunder

D. larceny (Larceny is similar to embezzlement, misappropriation, theft.)

-----

21. The use of drugs was <u>prevalent</u> in the 9th District.

A. common (Common is similar to prevalent, frequent, rampant.)

B. exceptional

C. scarce

D. limited

-----

22. The motive remained an <u>enigma</u> until the first day of trial.

A. certainty

B. mystery (Mystery is similar to enigma, puzzle, stumper.)

C. clearness

D. certainty

-----

23. Based on the witness accounts, the motive was <u>unequivocal</u>.

A. ambiguous

B. apparent (Apparent is similar to unequivocal, clear-cut, indisputable.)

C. unclear

D. vague

-----

24. Fueled by his drug abuse, his tears were <u>incessant</u>.

A. intermittent

B. unending (Unending is similar to incessant, endless, unrelenting.)

C. interrupted

D. broken

-----

25. The possibility of being discovered and punished was the major <u>deterrent</u> to committing the burglary.

A. assistance

B. encouragement

C. disincentive (Disincentive is similar to deterrent, discouragement, preventive.)

D. incentive

26. Although the charge was substantiated, his answers were <u>flippant</u>.

A. serious

B. courteous

C. respectful

D. frivolous (Frivolous is similar to flippant, flighty, impertinent.)

-----

27. The drugs were being processed by Elmore Labs and its <u>subsidiary</u>.

A. opponent

B. headquarters

C. branch (Branch is similar to subsidiary, partner company, auxiliary company.)

D. neighbor

-----

28. He gained the trust of the charitable contributors by appearing to be a <u>benevolent</u> person.

A. cruel

B. caring (Caring is similar to benevolent, benign, compassionate.)

C. miserly

D. malevolent

-----

29. When we extracted him from the rubble, his complexion was <u>pallid</u>.

A. healthy

B. hearty

C. strong

D. pale (Pale is similar to pallid, ashen, grey.)

-----

30. The heavy and bulky climbing equipment was a <u>hindrance</u> to the special officer.

A. aid

B. handicap (Handicap is similar to hindrance, impediment, interference.)

C. assistance

D. benefit

CALIFORNIA POST EXAM GUIDE (PELLETB)

Instructions: For the following questions 15 questions, (Questions 31-45), decide which sentence is most clearly written.

Choose "A" if sentence "a" is clearer than sentence "b".
Choose "B" if sentence "b" is clearer than sentence "a".

Question 31:

a. Seeing the robber head for the back door, adrenalin started flowing.

b. When he spotted the robber heading for the back door, the officer's adrenalin started flowing.

Answer 1: B (Sentence "a" does not make clear who saw the robber heading for the back door.)

Question 32:

a. Even the spectators across the street felt the blast of the explosion.

b. The spectators felt the blast of the explosion. Even the ones across the street.

Answer 2: A ("b" contains a sentence fragment, ""Even the ones across the street.")

Question 33:

a. The captain commended the officer for finding his missing hat.

b. The captain commended the officer for finding the captain's missing hat.

Answer 33: B ("a" is confusing because it is not clear whose hat is missing. The "his" in "his missing hat" does not make it clear whose hat is missing.)

Question 34:

a. The officer and the witness is on route to the court hearing.

b. The officer and the witness are on route to the court hearing.

Answer 34: B ("a" does not have subject/verb agreement. The subject "The captain and the witness" is a plural subject. The verb "is" is a singular verb.)

Question 35:

a. Because he used the van, the officer was able to transport the riot gear.

b. The officer was able to transport the riot gear. Because he used the van.

Answer 35: A ("b" contains the sentence fragment, "Because he used the van.")

CALIFORNIA POST EXAM GUIDE (PELLETB)

Question 36:

a. The fireworks show was on a small island in the middle of the wide river. The spectators were on the east side of the river.

b. The fireworks show was on a small island in the middle of the wide river, the spectators were on the east side of the river.

Answer 36: A ("b" is a run-on sentence.)

Question 37:

a. The mentally incompetent suspect confessed that he wanted everything he saw advertised, even though he often didn't understand what purpose they served.

b. The mentally incompetent suspect confessed that he wanted everything he saw advertised, even though he often didn't understand what purpose the items served.

Answer 37: B ("a" does not specify what the mentally incompetent person wanted.)

Question 38:

a. While breathing through their gas mask filters, the officers marched in a straight line.

b. The officers marched in a straight line. Breathing through their gas mask filters.

Answer 38: A ("b" contains a sentence fragment, "Breathing through their gas mask filters.")

Question 39:

a. After the officer and the victim spoke, he had a good idea.

b. After the officer spoke with the victim, the officer had a good idea.

Answer 39: B ("a" contains a reference error. It is not clear who "he" is referring to.)

Question 40:

a. The squad car made a rickety noise. It needed a tune-up.

b. The squad car made a rickety noise, it needed a tune-up.

Answer 40: A ("b" is a run-on sentence.)

Question 41:

a. Blowing out black fumes, Officer Follins called in a repair request.

b. Because the car was blowing out black fumes, Officer Follins called in a repair request.

CALIFORNIA POST EXAM GUIDE (PELLETB)

Answer 41: B ("a" has a reference error. It makes it seem like Officer Follins was blowing out black fumes.)

Question 42:

a. The items on the list of chores were long and difficult, especially the last four items.

b. The items on the list of chores were long and difficult. Especially the last four items.

Answer 42: A ("b" contains the sentence fragment, "Especially the last four items.")

Question 43:

a. Because the purple man's vase was broken in only two pieces, he had it glued back together.

b. Because the man's purple vase was broken in only two pieces, he had it glued back together.

Answer 43: B ('a" is clumsy. "the purple man's vase" should read, "the man's purple vase.")

Question 44:

a. He ate the spaghetti and drank red wine. Waiting for his employee to pick him up.

b. While waiting for his employee to pick him up, he ate spaghetti and drank red wine.

Answer 44: B ("a" contains the sentence fragment, " Waiting for his employee to pick him up.")

Question 45:

a. After placing the bracelet in a red pouch, she took it to her apartment.

b. After placing the bracelet in a red pouch, she took the pouch to her apartment.

Answer 45: B ("a" has a reference error. It does not make clear what specifically was taken to her apartment.)

For questions 46-47, read the following passage and then answer the questions based solely on the information provided in the passage.

"Terrorism" comes from the French word terrorisme, and originally referred specifically to state terrorism as practiced by the French government during the 1793–1794 Reign of Terror. The French word terrorisme in turn derives from the Latin verb terrere (e, terreo) meaning "to frighten". The Jacobins, coming to power in France in 1792, are said to have initiated the Reign of Terror (French: La Terreur). After the Jacobins lost power, the word "terrorist" became a term of abuse.

Although "terrorism" originally referred to acts committed by a government, currently it usually refers to the killing of innocent people for political purposes in such a way as to create a spectacle. This meaning can be traced back to Sergey Nechayev, who described himself as a "terrorist". Nechayev founded the Russian terrorist group "People's Retribution" in 1869.*

-----

46. Based on the preceding passage, which of the following statements is correct?

A. The word "terrorism" has always meant the same thing.

B. The Latin verb "terrere" derives from the French verb "terrorisme."

C. The Jacobins came to power in France in 1729.

D. The word "terrorist" became a term of abuse after the Jacobins lost power.

----

47. Based on the preceding passage, which of the following statements is not correct?

A. Sergey Nechayev, described himself as a "terrorist".

B. The Jacobins are said to have initiated the Reign of Terror.

C. "Terrorism" originally referred to acts committed by mobs of people.

(This is an incorrect statement. "Terrorism" originally referred to acts committed by a government.)

D. "Terrorism" comes from the French word terrorisme.

For questions 48-49, read the following passage and then answer the questions based solely on the information provided in the passage.

The lack of consensus as to what a terrorist is can affect policies designed to deal with terrorists. Some view them as soldiers that can be held at the end of a war and are entitled to various privileges spelled out in the Geneva Conventions. Others view them as criminals that should be tried in civil courts. Still others will argue that terrorists are best treated as a category to themselves and need policies tailored to them.

In November 2004, a Secretary-General of the United Nations report described terrorism as any act "intended to cause death or serious bodily harm to civilians or non-combatants with the purpose of intimidating a population or compelling a government or an international organization to do or abstain from doing any act".*

-----

48. According to the preceding passage, some people define terrorists as one of the following, except:

A. people in a category to themselves.

B. criminals

C. soldiers

D. politicians

----

49. According to the preceding passage, which of the following statements is not correct?

A. The title of the official of the United Nations mentioned in the passage is "Secretary-Genial."

(The correct title is "Secretary General.")

B. There is a lack of consensus as to what a terrorist is.

C. Some people view terrorists as criminals.

D. The terrorism report by the Secretary-General of the United Nations was dated November 2004.

For questions 50-51, read the following passage and then answer the questions based solely on the information provided in the passage.

The Glock pistol, sometimes referred to by the manufacturer as a Glock "Safe Action" pistol and colloquially as a Glock, is a series of polymer-framed, short recoil-operated, locked-breech semi-automatic pistols designed and produced by Glock Ges.m.b.H., located in Deutsch-Wagram, Austria. It entered Austrian military and police service by 1982 after it was the top performer on an exhaustive series of reliability and safety tests.

Despite initial resistance from the market to accept a "plastic gun" due to durability and reliability concerns, and fears, (subsequently shown to be unfounded), that the pistol would be "invisible" to metal detectors in airports, Glock pistols have become the company's most profitable line of products, commanding 65% of the market share of handguns for United States law enforcement agencies, as well as supplying numerous national armed forces, security agencies, and police forces in at least 48 countries. Glocks are also popular firearms among civilians for recreational and competition shooting, home and self-defense, and concealed carry or open carry.*

-----

50. Which of the following statements is not correct, according to the preceding paragraph?

A. Glock pistols have become the company's most profitable line of products.

B. Glock pistols have a 56% share of the market share of handguns for United States law enforcement agencies.

(The correct percentage is 65%.)

C. The Glock pistol is referred to colloquially as a Glock,

D. Glocks are also popular firearms among civilians for recreational and competition shooting.

----

51. According to the preceding passage, which of the following statements is not correct?

A. The Glock is referred to by the manufacturer as a Glock "Safe Action" pistol.

B. Metal pistols have become the company's most profitable line of products.

(This is not correct. In the passage, the Glock pistol is described as a "plastic gun.")

C. Glocks are used by police forces in 48 countries.

D. The Glock entered Austrian military and police service by 1982.

For questions 52-55, read the following passage and then answer the questions based solely on the information provided in the passage.

Concealed carry or carrying a concealed weapon (CCW), is the practice of carrying a weapon (such as a handgun) in public in a concealed manner, either on one's person or in close proximity. Not all weapons that fall under CCW laws are lethal. For example, in Florida, carrying pepper spray in more than a specified volume (2 oz.) of chemical requires a CCW permit, whereas anyone may legally carry a smaller, so-called, "self-defense chemical spray" device hidden on their person without a CCW permit.

There is no federal statutory law concerning the issuance of concealed-carry permits. All fifty states have passed laws allowing qualified individuals to carry certain concealed firearms in public, either without a permit or after obtaining a permit from a designated government authority at the state and/or local level. Vermont does not have such a statute but permits both open and concealed carry based on a court decision of long standing. Illinois had been the last state without such a provision – but its long-standing ban on concealed weapons was overturned in a federal appeals court, on Constitutional grounds. Illinois was ordered by the court to draft a concealed carry law by July 9, 2013 (including a 30-day extension) at which time the Illinois legislature, overriding the amendatory veto of the governor, approved legislation to permit and regulate concealed carry to begin by January 2014.*

-----

52. According to the above passage, which of the following statements is not correct?

A. All fifty states have passed laws allowing qualified individuals to carry certain concealed firearms in public.

B. In Florida, carrying pepper spray in more than a specified volume (2 oz.) of chemical requires a CCW permit.

C. All weapons that fall under CCW laws are lethal.

(This is not correct. It should read, " Not all weapons that fall under CCW laws are lethal.)

D. There is no federal statutory law concerning the issuance of concealed-carry permits.

----

53. According to the preceding passage, which of the following statements is not correct?

A. For example, in Florida, carrying pepper spray in more than a specified volume (2 oz.) of chemical requires a CCW permit,

B. Concealed carry or carrying a concealed weapon (CCW), is the practice of carrying a weapon (such as a handgun) in public in a concealed manner.

C. "In a public manner" is described as either on one's person or in close proximity.

D. There is no state statutory laws concerning the issuance of concealed-carry permits.

(This is not correct. It should read, "There is no federal statutory law concerning the issuance of concealed-carry permits.)

----

54. According to the preceding passage, "In a concealed manner" is defined as:

A. the practice of carrying a weapon in public in a concealed manner on one's person only.

B. the practice of carrying a weapon in public in a concealed manner in close proximity to the person only.

C. the practice of owning a weapon illegally.

D. the practice of carrying a weapon in public in a concealed manner, either on one's person or in close proximity.

(This is the correct answer. The definition is in the first sentence of the passage.)

----

55. According to the above passage, which of the following is a logical conclusion?

A. Puerto Rico does not have a law regarding concealed-carry permits.

B. All fifty states do not allow concealed weapons.

C. Vermont allows the carrying of concealed weapons.

("Vermont does not have such a statute but permits both open and concealed carry based on a court decision of long standing.")

D. The CCW is a private lobby group.

For questions 56-60, read the following passage and then answer the questions based solely on the information provided in the passage.

The California system has been the origin of many trends in prison conditions within the United States as a whole. The state's large and diverse population, large size, large urban areas, high rates of violent crime, criminal street gangs, tough sentencing laws and its status as an entry point to the U.S. for both immigrants and drugs has given California a large and complex prison environment. California prisons are overcrowded, with a number of facilities holding more than 200% of their design capacity.

The system, like the state as a whole, lacks a racial/ethnic majority among the population. Prisoner identification and affiliation is tied closely to race and region of the state, which has contributed to tension and violence. There has been a long running racial tension between African American and Southern Mexican American prison gangs and significant riots in California prisons where Mexican inmates and African Americans have targeted each other particularly, based on racial reasons. California is the birthplace of the United States' most powerful and well-known prison gangs, including the Aryan Brotherhood, Mexican Mafia, Nuestra Familia, and the Black Guerrilla Family. State efforts against these gangs made California a pioneer in the development of Security Housing Unit "supermax" control-unit facilities.

The overcrowded conditions and accusations of inadequate medical facilities and mistreatment have caused the federal courts to intervene in the system's operation since the 1990s, appointing special oversight and enforcing consent decrees over the system's medical system and the SHU units and capping populations at several facilities. As of 2007, by order of federal courts, the system's medical system is under federal receivership, and a federal court may impose a mandatory limit on the system's total inmate population.*

-----

56. According to the above passage:

A. The "Nusestra Familia" is a well-known prison gangs.

B. California prisons are not yet overcrowded.

C. Prisoner identification and affiliation is tied closely to race and region of the state.

(This is a direct quote of the second sentence in paragraph two.)

D. The system's medical system has received a federal commendation.

----

57. The federal court has done each of the following, except:

A. intervening in the system's operation.

B. appointing special oversight.

C. enforcing consent decrees.

D. releasing some prisoners to reduce overcrowding.

(This is not mentioned in the passage.)

----

58. California is the birthplace of the United States' of the following most powerful and well-known prison gangs, except:

A. Mexican Mafia

B. Aryan Brotherhood

C. Nuestra Famiglia.

D. Breaker Guerilla Family.

(This should read, <u>Black</u> Guerilla Family.)

----

59. Which of the following factors contributing to California's large and complex prison environment is not mentioned in the preceding passage?

A. high rates of violent crime

B. large urban areas

C. conservative judges.

(Judges are not mentioned in the passage.)

D. tough sentencing laws

----

60. According to the above passage:

A. Blacks make up the majority of the prison population.

B. Hispanics make up less than fifty percent of the prison population.

C. The prison system lacks a racial/ethnic majority among the population.

(This is said in the first sentence of the second paragraph.)

D. There is no tension between African American and Southern Mexican American prison gangs.

Instructions for Questions 61-105: In the following passages of text, certain words have been deleted and replaced by dashes (one dash for each letter of the word that has been deleted). Using the "contextual clues" in the paragraph, deduce the missing words and record your answers on the answer sheet, as instructed.

Passage 1:

The handgun 61) _ _ generally considered 62) _ _ _ smallest of all firearms. Single-shot pistols were used in historical times. However, today the 63) _ _ _ main categories of handguns 64) _ _ _ revolvers and semi-automatic pistols. Revolvers shoot single rounds drawn from one of the "charge holes" in a revolving cylinder. Semi-automatics draw their rounds 65) _ _ _ _ a magazine and can fire more than 66) _ _ _ round at a time.

Passage 2:

After arraignment and before entry of plea 67) _ _ guilty or commencement of trial, the court may upon motion of the people 68) _ _ defendant, or upon its own motion and consent of both the people and the defendant, order 69) _ _ ACD (ADJOURNMENT IN CONTEMPLATION OF DISMISSAL). 70) _ _ _ case is adjourned without 71) _ date. People may make an application 72) _ _ restore the case within 6 months. 73) _ _ that occurs, the court may restore it 74) _ _ _ proceed to trial. 75) _ _ the case is not restored, the accusatory instrument is deemed to have been dismissed in furtherance of justice at the end of the six-month period.

Passage 3:

Tardiness is the 76) _ _ _ _ _ _ _ _ of punctuality. To be punctual means to 77) _ _ on time, while tardiness means 78) _ _ _ habit of being late. In the United States, tardiness is frowned upon. In the workplace, 79) _ _ employee who is habitually tardy may 80) _ _ charged with misconduct 81) _ _ _ may be punished. 82) _ _ _ _ punishment may include demotion or termination of employment. However, not 83) _ _ _ cultures punish tardiness. 84) _ _ Africa, where a more relaxed lifestyle 85) _ _ preferred, tardiness is generally accepted as part of 86) _ _ _ lifestyle.

Passage 4:

When a criminal case 87) _ _ pending in 88) _ _ _ courts, the Police Officer who made the arrest 89) _ _ prohibited from discussing the case 90) _ _ _ _ any newspaper, magazine, TV reporters and all other media. Exceptions 91) _ _ this are 1) cases where a California court of competent jurisdiction formally orders the Police 92) _ _ _ _ _ _ _ to discuss one or more particulars of the case, 2) a California authorized Department orders such discussion, 3) the Police Officer 93) _ _ subpoenaed to testify by an authorized California State board 94) _ _ federal board.

Passage 5:

Police 95) _ _ _ _ _ _ _ _ Jack Ellis and Rhonda Cordan were 96) _ _ patrol on November 3, 2014 when at 7:15 p.m. 97) _ _ _ _ they witnessed a minor traffic accident (in front of 2455 Elmer Street, in Woodmere). Officer Ellis called 98) _ _ _ Police Dispatcher 99) _ _ 7:25 p.m. 100) _ _ _ reported that the two drivers 101) _ _ _ four passengers (102) (_ _ _ in each vehicle) did not sustain any personal injuries. 103) _ _ _ of the vehicles, the one driven 104) _ _ a male named Fred Ulmer, did have minor damage to the driver's side door, and the other vehicle, driven by a male named Oswald Trunger, had minor damage to 105) _ _ _ front bumper.

Answer for Questions 61-105:

61. is	76. opposite	91. to
62. the	77. be	92. Officer
63. two	78. the	93. is
64. are	79. an	94. or
65. from	80. be	95. Officers
66. one	81. and	96. on
67. of	82. this	97. when
68. or	83. all	98. the
69. an	84. in	99. at
70. the	85. is	100. and
71. a	86. the	101. and
72. to	87. is	102. two
73. if	88. the	103. one
74. and	89. is	104. by
75. if	90. with	105. the

Directions for Questions 106-110: In each of the following five questions, there is a number series. For each number series, you are to figure out the pattern in the series and determine what two numbers (represented by dashes) would be the last two numbers in the series.

-----

106)   53 30 51 28...49 26 ___ ___.

A) 45, 22   B) 47, 24   C) 55, 32   D) 45, 20

Answer 106: B (47, 24)

Pattern is two DOUBLE numbers (50 and 30) ALTERNATING and DECREASING by 2 each time.

----

107)   70 79 88 97 106 115 __ __

A) 122,131   B) 124, 134   C) 124, 135   D) 124, 133

Answer 107: D (124, 133)

Pattern is the number 70 INCREASING by 9 each time the pattern is repeated.

----

108)   2 6 18 54 __ __

A) 162, 486   B) 160, 484   C) 158, 488   D) 162, 484

Answer 108: A (162, 486)

Pattern is 2 MULTIPLIED by 3 each time the pattern is repeated (2 X 3 = 6, 6 X 3 = 18, 18 X 3 = 54, 54 X 3 = 162, 162 X 3 = 486).

----

109)   30 30 33 33 36 36 39 39 __ __

A) 46, 46   B) 42, 42   C) 48, 48   D) 46, 47

Answer 109: B (42, 42)

The pattern is the number 30 REPEATED once and then INCREASED by 3 each time the pattern is repeated (30, Repeat 30, 30 + 3 = 33, Repeat 33, 33 + 3 = 36, Repeat 36, 36 + 3 = 39, Repeat 39, 39 + 3 = 42, Repeat 42).

----

110)   93 84 76 69 63 58 __ __

A) 53, 51   B) 54, 51   C) 54, 52   D) 52, 53   E) 52, 51

Answer 110: B (54, 51)

The pattern is the number 93 DECREASING by a DECREASING number each time the pattern is repeated (93 - 9 = 84, 84 - 8 = 76, 76 - 7 = 69, 69 - 6 = 63, 63 - 5 = 58, 58 - 4 = 54, 54 - 3 = 51).

Directions: For questions 111-115, select the choice containing the word that does not belong in the group of the other three related words.

Question 111:

A. feast

B. celebration

C. gala

D. funeral (The other 3 words refer to happy, festive occasions. A "funeral" is a somber occasion.)

Question 112:

A. thicket

B. forest

C. woodland

D. clearing (The other 3 words refer to thick forest areas. A clearing refers to an area that is relatively clear.)

Question 113:

A. examination

B. inspection

C. instrument (The other 3 words refer to investigatory processes.)

D. probe

Question 114:

A. drink

B. libation

C. brew

D. steak (The other 3 words refer to liquid that are consumed. Steak is solid meat.)

Question 115:

A. old

B. aged

C. mature

D. embryonic (The other 3 words relate to older people. Embryonic refers to the period before birth.)

Question 116

Four firearms were found at the suspect's house. One firearm was a 45 caliber semi-automatic pistol. Another was a 38-caliber mini gun. Another was a home-made 12-caliber one-shot firearm. The other was a 50-caliber military weapon. Which of the following is the third highest caliber weapon found?

A. the military weapon

B. the mini-gun

C. the homemade on-shot firearm

D. the semi-automatic pistol

(The caliber order is: 1) the one-shot firearm (12 caliber), 2) the mini-gun (38 caliber), 3) the semi-automatic pistol (45 caliber), and 4) the military weapon (50 caliber).

Question 117

Your sergeant gives you five "Complaint Forms" with the following priority numbers:

9457   13647   0659   758   8793

He asks you to organize the forms in ascending priority.

According to the above, the third Complaint Form would be Complaint Form number:

A. 9457   C. 13647

B. 0758   **D. 8793**

The Complaint Forms in Ascending Priority Number Order are as follows:
1) 0659   2) 758   **3) 8793**   4) 9457   5) 13647
The third complaint number on the list is 8793. Therefore the correct answer is **D) 8793.**

Question 118

Your sergeant gives you five "Requests for Investigation" forms submitted by residents in your precinct. The forms were submitted by the following five persons:

1) James Vaccaro, 2) Carol Gomez, 3) William Jones, 4) Erika Whitfield, 5) Frances Diamond

He asks you to organize the forms in last name alphabetical order.

According to the above, the fourth "Request for Investigation" form is the one submitted by:

A. William, Jones

B. Vaccaro, James

C. Gomez, Carol

D. Whitfield, Erika

Answer 118

The correct listing in last name alphabetical order is:

1) Diamond, Frances

2) Gomez, Carol

3) Jones, William

4) Vaccaro, James

5) Whitfield, Erika

The fourth name on the list is Vaccaro, James, therefore the correct answer is **B. Vaccaro, James**

Question 118

Your sergeant gives you five "Requests for Investigation" forms submitted by residents in your precinct. The forms were submitted by the following five persons:

George Felder, Harriet Volker, Ben Halston, Abe Johnson, Diane Molton

He asks you to organize the forms in last name alphabetical order.

According to the above, the fourth "Request for Investigation" form is the one submitted by:

A. Halston, Ben

B. Volker, Harriet

C. Molton, Diane

D. Felder, George

Answer 118

The correct listing in last name alphabetical order is:

1) Felder, George

2) Halston, Ben

3) Johnson, Abe

4) Molton, Diane

5) Volker, Harriet

The fourth name on the list is Molton, Diane. The correct answer is <u>C) Molton, Diane.</u>

Directions for Questions 119-120: The following 2 questions are comprised of a series of sentences which are in scrambled order. Select the order of sentences (A, B, C, or D) which most correctly and logically places the sentences in a meaningful, logical, and effective order.

Question 119

1. Everyone is different, and there may be as many ways to study as there are people.

2. This does not mean, however, that all neural connections and all brains work alike.

3. Short sessions help the brain retain more, while studying over a period of time help to reinforce the neural connections in the brain.

4. Short study sessions over a long period of time are very helpful.

5. The manner and length of time that one practices answering questions can greatly affect the mark that one receives on an exam.

(A) 5-1-3-4-2

(B) 5-4-1-3-2

(C) 4-5-1-4-2

<u>(D) 5-4-3-2-1</u>

Answer 119: (D) 5-4-3-2-1

(5) The manner and length of time that one practices answering questions can greatly affect the mark that one receives on an exam.

(4) Short study sessions over a long period of time are very helpful.

(3) Short sessions help the brain retain more, while studying over a period of time help to reinforce the neural connections in the brain.

(2) This does not mean, however, that all neural connections and all brains work alike.

(1) Everyone is different, and there may be as many ways to study as there are people.

Question 120:

1. State permanent employees receive 20 days of paid vacation during their first year of service, in addition to 11 paid holidays.

2. The total of all these three types of benefit days is 54.

3. The State offers many types of benefits to its permanent employees.

4. They also accrue 13 days of paid annual sick leave.

5. In addition to pension benefits, it offers three types of paid days.

(A) 5-3-1-2-4

(B) 3-5-1-2-4

(C) 5-3-2-4-2

<u>**(D) 3-5-1-4-2**</u>

Answer 120: (D) 3-5-1-4-2

3. The State offers many types of benefits to its permanent employees.

5. In addition to pension benefits, it offers three types of paid days.

1. State permanent employees receive 20 days of paid vacation during their first year of service, in addition to 11 paid holidays.

4. They also accrue 13 days of paid annual sick leave.

2. The total of all these three types of benefit days is 54.

PRACTICE TEST 4 QUESTIONS 17

Instructions: For questions 1–15, select the choice with the correct spelling of the omitted word in the preceding sentence.

1. Because he didn't choose his words carefully, his _____ was unclear.

A. riting

B. writting

C. writeing

D. writing

-----

2. Because of the accident, the _____ was a complete loss.

A. veical

B. vihicle

C. vehicle

D. vehecel

-----

3. _____ alibi was was proven to be untrue.

A. There

B. Their

C. They're

D. Thier

-----

4. The officer _____ them because they were still arguing.

A. separated

B. seperated

C. separeted

D. sepparated

-----

5. The attorney made a _____ to Article 10 of the criminal law.

A. referance

B. reference

C. referrence

D. refrence

-----

6. The _____ of a controlled substance charge was dismissed.

A. posesssion

B. possesion

C. possession

D. posesion

-----

7. It took a great deal of _____ to uncover the evidence.

A. perseverance

B. persaverance

C. perseverence

D. persevverance

-----

8. He waited for a special _____ to give her the gift.

A. ocasion

B. ocassion

C. occassion

D. occasion

-----

9. The last time he had visited was during the month of _____.

A. Febuery

B. February

C. Febreury

D. Febbuary

-----

10. He was _____ because he didn't have any drugs.

A. desparate

B. desperrate

C. desperate

D. desparete

-----

11. She said that it was an _____ way to act.

A. awfull

B. awful

C. auful

D. aweful

-----

12. He said he ran away _____ he was afraid to be alone.

A. beccose

B. beccause

C. becous

D. because

-----

13. He was _____ sick to got to work.

A. two

B. to

C. tuh

D. too

-----

14. He got into trouble because of his _____ personality.

A. agressive

B. aggressive

C. agresive

D. aggresive

15. He _____ that he had been at the scene of the crime.

A. acknowledged

B. aknowledged

C. acknoledged

D. acknoladged

Instructions: For questions 16-30, choose the word that is closest in meaning to the underlined word in the sentence.

16. The empty office was <u>vandalized</u> by three teenagers.

A. mended

B. repaired

C. fixed

D. damaged

-----

17. He was easily confused by the offer because he was <u>illiterate</u>.

A. intelligent

B. uneducated

C. learned

D. able

-----

18. For the first few minutes after he gained consciousness, he was <u>incoherent</u>.

A. connected

B. intelligible

C. understandable

D. incomprehensible

-----

19. All the electronic equipment made the emergency back-pack <u>cumbersome</u>.

A. compact

B. burdensome

C. convenient

D. graceful

-----

20. He remained for a week in the hospital because the <u>laceration</u> was serious.

A. sunburn

B. gash

C. irritation

D. medication

-----

21. The political boss had a reputation as being a <u>formidable</u> enemy.

A. powerful

B. weak

C. ineffectual

D. anemic

-----

22. The officer <u>admonished</u> the spectator for jumping over the fence.

A. extolled

B. touted

C. lauded

D. reprimanded

-----

23. The suspect confessed that his intention had been to damage the motorcycle <u>adjacent</u> to the one that actually got damaged.

A. away

B. farthest

C. closest

D. distant

-----

24. When Officer Johnson arrived at the scene, he was <u>apprised</u> of the situation by Officer Brown who had witnessed the incident.

A. misinformed

B. misled

C. informed

D. deceived

-----

25. He considered the comment to be a <u>defamation</u> of his character.

A. commendation

B. approval

C. disparagement

D. commendation

-----

26. The alcoholic drink she was offered made her very lethargic.

A. active

B. drowsy

C. alert

D. animated

-----

27. The offender was handcuffed because he acted in a belligerent manner.

A. pacific

B. combative

C. uncontentious

D. peaceful

-----

28. The celebration was boisterous, so the neighbor complained to the police.

A. noisy

B. sedate

C. quiet

D. noiseless

-----

29. After a second trial, the defendant was exonerated.

A. condemned

B. sentenced

C. acquitted

D. convicted

-----

30. The suspect confessed that he was enamored with the complainant.

A. embittered

B. repulsed

C. soured

D. enchanted

Instructions: For the following questions 15 questions, (Questions 31-45), decide which sentence is most clearly written.

Choose "A" if sentence "a" is clearer than sentence "b".

Choose "B" if sentence "b" is clearer than sentence "a".

Question 31:

a. The informant was seated at the table, he was very helpful.

b. The very helpful informant was seated at the table.

Question 32:

a. The victim pointed to the student who looked like the attacker in the class picture.

b. The victim pointed to the student in the picture who looked like the attacker.

Question 33:

a. The officer instructed the driver to take his driver's license out of his wallet and place it on the seat.

b. The officer instructed the driver to take his driver's license out of his wallet and place the license on the seat.

Question 34:

a. The shoppers escaped from the side entrance. The workers followed.

b. The shoppers escaped from the side entrance, the workers followed.

Question 35:

a. The officer spotted the gold man's watch that was reported stolen.

b. The officer spotted the man's gold watch that was reported stolen.

Question 36:

a. The volunteers took the cookies to the homeless shelter, where they were very much welcomed.

b. The volunteers took the cookies to the homeless shelter. Very much welcomed.

Question 37:

a. The witness threw out the toy, which was a mistake.

b. The witness made the mistake of throwing out the toy.

Question 38:

a. The boxes were scattered in the parking lot. The tools were piled in front of the entrance.

b. The boxes were scattered in the parking lot, the tools were piled in front of the entrance.

Question 39:

a. Because of the "certain look," the gang members realized he had figured out their scheme.

b. Because of the "certain look" from the officer, the gang members realized he had figured out their scheme.

Question 40:

a. The officer picked up the silver dirty pin from the floor.

b. The officer picked up the dirty silver pin from the floor.

Question 41:

a. Seeing the child running away from her attacker, the officer's heart skipped in joy.

b. The officer's heart skipped in joy. Seeing the child running away from her attacker.

Question 42:

a. Even the rookie officers volunteered for overtime duty.

b. The officers volunteered for overtime duty. Even the rookie officers.

Question 43:

a. The store owner thanked the sergeant for finding his missing pepper spray.

b. The store owner thanked the sergeant for finding the store owner's missing pepper spray.

Question 44:

a. Aided by the rookies, the senior officer completed the report on time.

b. The senior officer completed the report on time. Aided by the rookies.

Question 45:

a. The officer put the gun in a box and told the rookie to take it to the evidence room.

b. The officer put the gun in a box and told the rookie to take the box to the evidence room.

For question 46, read the following passage and then answer the question based solely on the information provided in the passage.

A uniform is a type of clothing worn by members of an organization while participating in that organization's activity. Modern uniforms are most often worn by armed forces and paramilitary organizations such as police, emergency services, security guards, in some workplaces and schools and by inmates in prisons. In some countries, some other officials also wear uniforms in their duties; such is the case of the Commissioned Corps of the United States Public Health Service or the French prefects. For some public groups, such as police, it is illegal for non-members to wear the uniform. Other uniforms are trade dresses (such as the brown uniforms of UPS).*

46. According to the above passage:

A. Modern uniforms are most often worn by non-military organizations.

B. UPS uniforms are beige.

C. For some public groups, such as police, it is illegal for non-members to wear the uniform.

D. Schools must obtain permission for students to wear uniforms.

For question 47, read the following passage and then answer the question based solely on the information provided in the passage.

A vacation or holiday is a leave of absence from a regular occupation, or a specific trip or journey, usually for the purpose of recreation or tourism. People often take a vacation during specific holiday observances, or for specific festivals or celebrations. Vacations are often spent with friends or family.

A person may take a longer break from work, such as a sabbatical, gap year, or career break.

The concept of taking a vacation is a recent invention, and has developed through the last two centuries. Historically, the idea of travel for recreation was a luxury that only wealthy people could afford. In the Puritan culture of early America, taking a break from work for reasons other than weekly observance of the Sabbath was frowned upon. However, the modern concept of vacation was led by a later religious movement encouraging spiritual retreat and recreation. The notion of breaking from work periodically took root among the middle and working class.*

47. Which of the following statements is not supported by the preceding paragraph?

A. A sabbatical is a short break from work.

B. People often take a vacation during specific holiday observances.

C. Vacations are often spent with friends or family.

D. The concept of taking a vacation is a recent invention.

For questions 48-50, read the following passage and then answer the questions based solely on the information provided in the passage.

The states use different terminology for licenses or permits to carry a concealed firearm, such as a Concealed Handgun License/Permit (CHL/CHP), Concealed Carry Weapons (CCW), Concealed (Defensive/Deadly) Weapon Permit/License (CDWL/CWP/CWL), Concealed Carry Permit/License (CCP/CCL), License to Carry (Firearms) (LTC/LTCF), Carry of Concealed Deadly Weapon license (CCDW), Concealed Pistol License (CPL), etc. Thirteen states use a single permit to regulate the practices of both concealed and open carry of a handgun.

Some states publish statistics indicating how many residents hold permits to carry concealed weapons, and their demographics. For example, Florida has issued 2,031,106 licenses since adopting its law in 1987, and had 843,463 licensed permit holders as of July 31, 2011. It is likely that by December 2012 Florida had reached the milestone of 1 million active licensees within a population of 19 million. Reported permit holders are predominantly male. Some states have reported the number of permit holders increasing over time. "With hard numbers or estimates from all but three of the 49 states that have laws allowing for issuance of carry permits, the U.S. Government Accountability Office reports that there were about 8 million active permits in the United States as of December 31, 2011. That's about a million more than previous estimates by scholars.*

-----

48. Which of the following is not included in the terms used by states to refer to licenses or permits to carry a concealed firearm?

A. License to Carry (Firearms) (LTC/LTCF)

B. Concealed Carry Weapons (CCW)

C. Concealed Pistol License (CPL)

D. Carry of Concealed Non-Deadly Weapon license (CCDW)

----

49. How many states use a single permit to regulate the practices of both concealed and open carry of a handgun?

A. less than 10

B. thirteen

C. more than 19t

D. fifteen

----

50. According to the preceding passage:

A. For example, Florida has issued 2,013,106 licenses since adopting its law in 1987, and had 843,463 licensed permit holders as of July 31, 2011.

B. For example, Florida has issued 2,031,106 licenses since adopting its law in 1987, and had 843,463 licensed permit holders as of July 31, 2001.

C. For example, Florida has issued 2,031,106 licenses since adopting its law in 1987, and had 843,463 licensed permit holders as of July 31, 2011.

D. For example, Florida has issued 2,031,106 licenses since adopting its law in 1978, and had 843,463 licensed permit holders as of July 31, 2011.

For questions 51-53, read the following passage and then answer the questions based solely on the information provided in the passage.

Crowd control is a public security practice where large crowds are managed to prevent the outbreak of crowd crushes, affray, fights involving drunk and disorderly people or riots. Crowd crushes in particular can cause many hundreds of fatalities. Crowd control can involve privately hired security guards as well as police officers. Crowd control is often used at large, public gatherings like street fairs, music festivals, stadiums and public demonstrations. At some events, security guards and police use metal detectors and sniffer dogs to prevent weapons and drugs being brought into a venue.

Materials such as stanchions, crowd control barriers, fences and decals painted on the ground can be used to direct a crowd. Keeping the crowd comfortable and relaxed is also essential, so things like awnings, cooling fans (in hot weather), and entertainment are sometimes used as well.

Specific products that are used to implement line management and public guidance in high traffic areas include retractable belt systems (which incorporate a stanchion post and the retractable tape) and wall mount systems (also incorporating a retractable belt but are surface mounted). Post and rope systems are also popular, especially in banks and theaters.*

-----

51. According to the above passage:

A. Crowd control only involve police officers.

B. Crowd control does not involve any equipment.

C. Crowd control does not use sniffer dogs if metal detectors are available.

D. Crowd control can involve privately hired security guards as well as police officers.

----

52. Which of the following is not supported by the preceding passage?

A. Crowd often form after sunset.

B. Small crowds are often deadlier than large crowds.

C. Crowd crushes can cause many hundreds of fatalities.

D. Crowd control training must be increased.

----

53. Which of the following statements is supported by the above paragraph?

A. At all events, security guards and police use metal detectors and sniffer dogs to prevent weapons and drugs being brought into a venue.

B. At some events, security guards and police use metal detectors and sniffer dogs to prevent weapons and drugs being removed from a venue.

C. At some events, security guards and police use metal detectors and sniffer dogs to prevent food from being brought into a venue.

D. At some events, security guards and police use metal detectors and sniffer dogs to prevent weapons and drugs being brought into a venue.

For questions 54-55, read the following passage and then answer the questions based solely on the information provided in the passage.

In non-military law enforcement, patrol officers are law enforcement officers assigned to monitor specified geographic areas—that is, to move through their areas at regular intervals looking out for any signs of problems of any kind. They are the officers most commonly encountered by the public, as their duties include responding to calls for service, making arrests, resolving disputes, taking crime reports, and conducting traffic enforcement, and other crime prevention measures. A patrol officer is often the first to arrive on the scene of any incident; what such an officer does or fails to do at the scene can greatly influence the outcome of any subsequent investigation. The patrol officer, as the person who is in the field daily, is often closest to potential crime and may have developed contacts who can provide information.*

-----

54. According to the preceding passage:

A. Special officers are the officers most commonly encountered by the public

B. Detectives are usually the first to arrive on the scene of any incident.

C. Sergeants are the persons who are in the field daily.

D. To patrol means to move through an area at regular intervals looking out for any signs of problems.

----

55. According to the preceding passage, the duties of a patrol officer include all the following, except:

A. taking crime reports

B. officiating at political rallies

C. conducting traffic enforcement

D. resolving disputes

For questions 56-60, read the following passage and then answer the questions based solely on the information provided in the passage.

The United States police rank model is generally quasi-militaristic in structure. Much like the London Metropolitan Police, there are enlisted, non-commissioned, officer, and general officer grades. A uniform system of insignia based on that of the US Army and Marine Corps is used to help identify an officer's seniority.

Chief of police/police commissioner/superintendent/sheriff: The title police commissioner is used mainly by large metropolitan departments, while chief of police is associated with small and medium-sized municipalities; both are typically appointed by a mayor or selected by the city council or commission. In some cities, "commissioner" is the member of the board of officials in charge of the department, while a "chief" is the top uniformed officer answering to the commissioner or commission. In very large departments, such as the New York City Police Department, there may be several non-police officer deputy and assistant commissioners, some of whom outrank the chief of department and others on par with the uniformed chief. There may be a chief of operations who is second in command to the top-ranking chief. In contrast, sheriffs in the United States are usually elected officials, one in each county, who head the sheriff's department (or sheriff's office).

Assistant Chief of Police/Assistant Commissioner/Assistant Superintendent: Only seen in some departments. In New York City, assistant chiefs head borough commands.

Deputy Chief of Police/Deputy Commissioner/Deputy Superintendent/Chief Deputy/undersheriff: The top subordinate of the chief of police, commissioner, superintendent, or sheriff; may or may not have a specific area of responsibility. In some places the undersheriff is the warden of the county jail. The New York City Sheriff's Office has five undersheriffs: each one is responsible for a borough of New York City, with the Sheriff of the City of New York overseeing all of them.

Inspector/commander: Sometimes have an insignia of a single star, analogous to brigadier generals, but in other areas wear a gold or silver eagle, similar to a colonel. "Inspector" is also used as a term for "detective" in the San Francisco Police Department but is two ranks above captain in the NYPD and the Philadelphia Police Department. In the NYPD, Inspectors command divisions, which may be groups of precincts within a borough or specialized branches of the police service.

Colonel: A majority of state police agencies use "colonel" as their senior executive rank, often jointly with a civilian title such as "superintendent," "commissioner" or "director." Conversely, the colonel rank is rarely employed by other agencies, though it is used by the Baltimore Police Department and other Maryland agencies as either an executive or commander-like rank. Colonels generally wear the gold or silver eagle of a colonel, or the oak leaf of a lieutenant colonel, from the U.S. armed forces. Many sheriffs also wear the eagle insignia, and use colonel as an official rank.

Major/deputy inspector: Sometimes have an insignia of a gold or silver oak leaf, similar to a major or lieutenant colonel. In the Baltimore Police Department and Atlanta Police Department majors supervise police stations.*

-----

56. Which of the following is not supported by the preceding passage?

A. Colonels generally wear a gold or silver eagle, or an oak leaf.

B. Major/deputy inspector sometimes have an insignia of a gold or silver oak leaf.

C. Chief of Police sometimes wear five stars.

D. Inspector/commander sometimes have an insignia of a single star.

----

57. Which of the following statements is not supported by the preceding paragraph?

A. Inspectors/commanders are analogous to brigadier generals.

B. Inspectors/commanders sometimes wear a gold or silver eagle, similar to a colonel.

C. Inspectors command divisions, which may be groups of precincts within a borough or specialized branches of the police service.

D. "Inspector" is also used as a term for "detective" in the New York Police Department.

----

58. Which of the following statements is not supported by the preceding paragraph?

A. A majority of state police agencies use "colonel" as their senior executive rank.

B. A majority of state police agencies often use "colonel" jointly with a civilian title such as "superintendent," "commissioner" or "director."

C. "Colonel" is used by the Baltimore Police Department and other Maryland agencies as either an executive or commander-like rank.

D. Colonels generally wear the gold or silver eagle of a colonel, or the oak leaf of a lieutenant colonel, patterned from the New York Police Department.

----

59. Which of the following police rank is not discussed in the preceding passage?

A. Inspector

B. Major

C. patrolman

D. Commander

----

60. According to the preceding passage, a uniform system of insignia based on that of the US Army and Marine Corps is used to help identify:

A. age of uniformed person

B. number of commendations

C. number of successful campaigns

D. an officer's seniority

Instructions for Questions 61-105: In the following passages of text, certain words have been deleted and replaced by dashes (one dash for each letter of the word that has been deleted). Using the "contextual clues" in the paragraph, deduce the missing words and record your answers on the answer sheet, as instructed.

Passage 1:

On Tuesday, his first day 61) _ _ the job 62) _ _ Queens County, while Police Officer Jane Sanchez called 63) _ _ _ an ambulance, Kevin administered emergency first aid on 64) _ _ elderly woman who had fainted 65) _ _ _ cut her forehead 66) _ _a court chair. 67) _ _ _ Police Officer assigned to 68) _ _ _ Part, Agnes Milliken, assisted Kevin in lifting the woman from the floor. The ambulance arrived at 11:10 A.M., five minutes after Police Officer Sanchez called 911. The EMT's examined the woman 69) _ _ _ determined that her breathing was unusually labored. They administered oxygen, placed her 70) _ _ a stretcher and rushed 71) _ _ _ to Queens Mercy Hospital, at 45 Brighton Avenue, about twelve blocks away 72) _ _ _ _ the courthouse.

Passage 1:

Police uniforms 73) _ _ many foreign countries 74) _ _ _ the same throughout the country. However, 75) _ _ the United States, the uniforms differ from 76) _ _ _ area to another. 77) _ _ _ _ variety is primarily 78) _ _ _ result of the many decentralized jurisdictions in the 79) _ _ _ _ _ states. Although dissimilar, all uniforms share certain characteristics. All of them 80) _ _ _ designed to present a sharp 81) _ _ _ professional appearance, and they are all designed to make the officers easily identifiable to 82) _ _ _ public and fellow officers.*

Passage 2:

Police Officer Trainees receive approximately two months of training at the Police Officers Academy, located at 87 Windham Street. The majority 83) _ _ the training is done in a classroom setting. 84) _ _ the classroom setting, trainees receive instruction 85) _ _ such matters 86) _ _ public relations, criminal statutes, court procedures, first aid 87) _ _ _ crowd control. Training and qualification 88) _ _ the Glock semi-automatic 89) _ _ _ done at 90) _ _ _ firing range located 91) _ _ 12 Leonard Street. Following the academy training, 92) _ _ _ _ _ _ Officer Trainees are assigned 93) _ _ a specific court where they are further trained in the security 94) _ _ _ clerical procedures of that court. Although 95) _ _ _ _ _ _ Officers are primarily responsible 96) _ _ _ security, knowledge of court 97) _ _ _ clerical procedures help them to understand the court process and help them to better serve 98) _ _ _ public.

The right 99) _ _ appeal a judicial order is 100) _ _ important right for all Americans. During an appeal, both the decision of 101) _ _ _ court and the actual law 102) _ _ _ reviewed. This right to appeal was first recognized during the first dynasty of Babylon, 103) _ _ _ _ King Hammurabi and his governors served as the "appellate courts." Today, almost 104) _ _ _ democratic countries have an appeals process. It is only in dictatorial or oligarchic nations 105) _ _ _ _ the right to appeal is non-existent.*

_____

Directions for Questions 106-110: In each of the following five questions, there is a number series. For each number series, you are to figure out the pattern in the series and determine what two numbers (represented by dashes) would be the last two numbers in the series.

-----

106)   109 73 105 69...101 65 ___ ___.

A) 97, 61   B) 95, 59   C) 99, 61   D) 97, 63

----

107)   57 72 87 102 117 132 __ __

A) 145, 162   B) 149, 164   C) 143, 162   D) 147, 162

----

108)   1 3 9 27 __ __

A) 81, 242   B) 80, 243   C) 79, 247   D) 81, 244   E) 81, 243

----

109)   60 64 68 72 76 80 84 88 __ __

A) 92, 96   B) 90, 94   C) 94, 98   D) 91, 95

----

110)   93 84 76 69 63 58 __ __

A) 53, 51   B) 54, 51   C) 54, 52   D) 52, 53   E) 52, 51

Answer 110: B (54, 51)

Directions: For questions 111-115, select the choice containing the word that does not belong in the group of the other three related words.

Question 111:

A. hosiery

B. socks

C. nylons

D. hat

Question 112:

A. jail

B. penitentiary

C. reformatory

D. courtroom

Question 113:

A. bracelet

B. necklace

C. eyeglasses

D. pendant

Question 114:

A. church

B. synagogue

C. chapel

D. auditorium

Question 115:

A. crook

B. hustler

C. cheater

D. statesman

CALIFORNIA POST EXAM GUIDE (PELLETB)

Question 116

Four screwdrivers used in burglaries were discovered at the suspect's house. One was silver in color and 16 inches long. One was blue and eight inches long. One was red and 12 inches long. One was yellow and fourteen inches long. What color was the third longest screwdriver?

A. blue

B. yellow

C. red

D. silver

Question 117

Your sergeant gives you five "Complaint Forms" with the following priority numbers:

5293   14275   0698   879   7892

He asks you to organize the forms in ascending priority.

According to the above, the third Complaint Form would be Complaint Form number:

A. 14275   C. 5293

B. 0698   D. 879

Question 118

Your sergeant gives you five "Requests for Investigation" forms submitted by residents in your precinct. The forms were submitted by the following five persons:

1) Norman Dankin, 2) Leon Cohen, 3) Frank Warden, 4) Michael Forman, 5) Harriet Russfield

He asks you to organize the forms in last name alphabetical order.

According to the above, the fourth "Request for Investigation" form is the one submitted by:

A. Warden, Frank

B. Russfield, Harry

C. Dankin, Norman

D. Forman, Michael

Directions for Questions 119-120: The following 2 questions are comprised of a series of sentences which are in scrambled order. Select the order of sentences (A, B, C, or D) which most correctly and logically places the sentences in a meaningful, logical, and effective order.

Question 119:

1. If you belong to the exempt group, you must have proper documentation and ID.

2. The announcement also contains a section regarding the exam fee waiver.

3. A combined filing and processing fee is required for this examination.

4. Everyone must pay the fee unless they are exempt by law.

5. The amount of the fee is noted on the examination announcement.

(A) 5-3-4-2-1

(B) 3-5-2-4-1

(C) 3-2-5-4-1

(D) 3-5-2-1-4

Question 120:

1. Among these benefits are dental and optical benefits.

2. If you add to this amount, life insurance and other benefits, the total possible yearly benefit may exceed six or seven thousand dollars per family.

3. Court Assistants and Court Officers are represented by the New York State Court Officer's Association.

4. The combined amount of these two types of benefits may be two thousand dollars per year for each family member.

5. This association provides many quality benefits to its employees.

(A) 3-5-1-4-2

(B) 5-3-4-1-2

(C) 4-5-1-4-2

(D) 3-1-5-4-2

PRACTICE TEST 4 ANSWERS   18

Instructions: For questions 1–15, select the choice with the correct spelling of the omitted word in the preceding sentence.

1.Because he didn't choose his words carefully, his _____ was unclear.

A. riting

B. writting

C. writeing

D. writing

-----

2. Because of the accident, the _____ was a complete loss.

A. veical

B. vihicle

C. vehicle

D. vehecel

-----

3. _____ alibi was was proven to be untrue.

A. There

B. Their

C. They're

D. Their

-----

4. The officer _____ them because they were still arguing.

A. separated

B. seperated

C. separeted

D. sepparated

-----

5. The attorney made a _____ to Article 10 of the criminal law.

A. referance

B. reference

C. referrence

D. refrence

-----

6. The _____ of a controlled substance charge was dismissed.

A. posesssion

B. possesion

C. possession

D. posesion

-----

7. It took a great deal of _____ to uncover the evidence.

A. perseverance

B. persaverance

C. perseverence

D. persevverance

-----

8. He waited for a special _____ to give her the gift.

A. ocasion

B. ocassion

C. occassion

D. occasion

-----

9. The last time he had visited was during the month of _____.

A. Febuery

B. February

C. Febreury

D. Febbuary

-----

10. He was _____ because he didn't have any drugs.

A. desparate

B. desperrate

C. desperate

D. desparete

-----

11. She said that it was an _____ way to act.

A. awfull

B. awful

C. auful

D. aweful

-----

12. He said he ran away _____ he was afraid to be alone.

A. beccose

B. beccause

C. becous

D. because

-----

13. He was _____ sick to got to work.

A. two

B. to

C. tuh

D. too

-----

14. He got into trouble because of his _____ personality.

A. agressive

B. aggressive

C. agresive

D. aggresive

15. He _____ that he had been at the scene of the crime.

A. acknowledged

B. aknowledged

C. acknoledged

D. acknoladged

Instructions: For questions 16-30, choose the word that is closest in meaning to the underlined word in the sentence.

16. The empty office was <u>vandalized</u> by three teenagers.

A. mended

B. repaired

C. fixed

D. damaged (Damaged is similar to smash, wreck, disfigure.)

-----

17. He was easily confused by the offer because he was <u>illiterate</u>.

A. intelligent

B. uneducated (Uneducated is similar to illiterate, uninstructed, unschooled.)

C. learned

D. able

-----

18. For the first few minutes after he gained consciousness, he was <u>incoherent</u>.

A. connected

B. intelligible

C. understandable

D. incomprehensible (Incomprehensible is similar to incongruous, inarticulate, rambling.)

-----

19. All the electronic equipment made the emergency back-pack <u>cumbersome</u>.

A. compact

B. burdensome (Burdensome is similar to cumbersome, inconvenient, unwieldy.)

C. convenient

D. graceful

-----

20. He remained for a week in the hospital because the <u>laceration</u> was serious.

A. sunburn

B. gash (Gash is similar to laceration, gash, slash.)

C. irritation

D. medication

CALIFORNIA POST EXAM GUIDE (PELLETB)

21. The political boss had a reputation as being a <u>formidable</u> enemy.

A. powerful (Powerful is similar to formidable, tough, tremendous.)

B. weak

C. ineffectual

D. anemic

-----

22. The officer <u>admonished</u> the spectator for jumping over the fence.

A. extolled

B. touted

C. lauded

D. reprimanded (Admonished is similar to reprimanded, rebuked, scolded.)

-----

23. The suspect confessed that his intention had been to damage the motorcycle <u>adjacent</u> to the one that actually got damaged.

A. away

B. farthest

C. closest (Adjacent and closest both mean abutting, neighboring, or flanking. Away, farthest, and distant indicate far away from the car.)

D. distant

-----

24. When Officer Johnson arrived at the scene, he was <u>apprised</u> of the situation by Officer Brown who had witnessed the incident.

A. misinformed

B. misled

C. informed (Apprised and informed both mean being told about something. Misinformed, misled, and deceived are contrary to the meaning of informed.)

D. deceived

-----

25. He considered the comment to be a <u>defamation</u> of his character.

A. commendation

B. approval

C. disparagement (Disparagement is similar to defamation, smear, denigration.)

D. commendation

26. The alcoholic drink she was offered made her very <u>lethargic</u>.

A. active

<u>B. drowsy</u> (Drowsy is similar to lethargic, sleepy, inactive.)

C. alert

D. animated

-----

27. The offender was handcuffed because he acted in a <u>belligerent</u> manner.

A. pacific

<u>B. combative</u> (Pacific, uncontentious, and peaceful are nonaggressive ways to act, the opposite of belligerent.)

C. uncontentious

D. peaceful

-----

28. The celebration was <u>boisterous</u>, so the neighbor complained to the police.

<u>A. noisy</u> (Sedate, quiet, and noiseless all express calmness, the opposite of boisterous.)

B. sedate

C. quiet

D. noiseless

-----

29. After a second trial, the defendant was <u>exonerated</u>.

A. condemned

B. sentenced

<u>C. acquitted</u> (Acquitted is similar to exonerated, absolved, vindicated.)

D. convicted

-----

30. The suspect confessed that he was <u>enamored</u> with the complainant.

A. embittered

B. repulsed

C. soured

<u>D. enchanted</u> (Enchanted is similar to enamored, captivated, enraptured.)

CALIFORNIA POST EXAM GUIDE (PELLETB)

Instructions: For the following questions 15 questions, (Questions 31-45), decide which sentence is most clearly written.

Choose "A" if sentence "a" is clearer than sentence "b".
Choose "B" if sentence "b" is clearer than sentence "a".

Question 31:

a. The informant was seated at the table, he was very helpful.

b. The very helpful informant was seated at the table.

Answer 31: B ("a" is a run-on sentence.)

Question 32:

a. The victim pointed to the student who looked like the attacker in the class picture.

b. The victim pointed to the student in the picture who looked like the attacker.

Answer 32: B ("b" is smoother and does not have the modification error that "a" has.)

Question 33:

a. The officer instructed the driver to take his driver's license out of his wallet and place it on the seat.

b. The officer instructed the driver to take his driver's license out of his wallet and place the license on the seat.

Answer 33: B ("a" has a reference error. It does not state clearly what the driver should place on the seat.)

Question 34:

a. The shoppers escaped from the side entrance. The workers followed.

b. The shoppers escaped from the side entrance, the workers followed.

Answer 34: A ("b" is a run-on sentence.)

Question 35:

a. The officer spotted the gold man's watch that was reported stolen.

b. The officer spotted the man's gold watch that was reported stolen.

Answer 35: B ("a" has a modification error. The correct version of "gold man's watch" is "man's gold watch".)

Question 36:

a. The volunteers took the cookies to the homeless shelter, where they were very much welcomed.

b. The volunteers took the cookies to the homeless shelter. Very much welcomed.

Answer 36: A ('b" has the sentence fragment, "Very much welcomed." The fragment contains the verb "welcomed", but it does not state what was welcomed.)

Question 37:

a. The witness threw out the toy, which was a mistake.

b. The witness made the mistake of throwing out the toy.

Answer 37: B ("a" contains a reference error. "Which was a mistake" does not make clear what was a mistake: the witness throwing out the toy OR the toy itself?)

Question 38:

a. The boxes were scattered in the parking lot. The tools were piled in front of the entrance.

b. The boxes were scattered in the parking lot, the tools were piled in front of the entrance.

Answer 38: A ("b" is a run-on sentence.)

Question 39:

a. Because of the "certain look," the gang members realized he had figured out their scheme.

b. Because of the "certain look" from the officer, the gang members realized he had figured out their scheme.

Answer 39: B ("a" has a modification error. Sentence "a" is confusing as to who has that "certain look" - the gang members or the police officer?)

Question 40:

a. The officer picked up the silver dirty pin from the floor.

b. The officer picked up the dirty silver pin from the floor.

Answer 40: B ("a" has a misplaced modifier. A "dirty silver pin" is smoother and clearer than " silver dirty pin.")

Question 41:

a. Seeing the child running away from her attacker, the officer's heart skipped in joy.

b. The officer's heart skipped in joy. Seeing the child running away from her attacker.

Answer 41: A ("b" contains the sentence fragment, " Seeing the child running away from her attacker.")

Question 42:

a. Even the rookie officers volunteered for overtime duty.

b. The officers volunteered for overtime duty. Even the rookie officers.

Answer 42: A ("b" contains a sentence fragment, "Even the rookie officers.")

Question 43:

a. The store owner thanked the sergeant for finding his missing pepper spray.

b. The store owner thanked the sergeant for finding the store owner's missing pepper spray.

Answer43: B ("a" is confusing because it is not clear whose pepper spray is missing. The "his" in "his pepper spray" does not make it clear whose pepper spray it is.)

Question 44:

a. Aided by the rookies, the senior officer completed the report on time.

b. The senior officer completed the report on time. Aided by the rookies.

Answer 44: A ("b" contains the sentence fragment, " Aided by the rookies.")

Question 45:

a. The officer put the gun in a box and told the rookie to take it to the evidence room.

b. The officer put the gun in a box and told the rookie to take the box to the evidence room.

Answer 45: B ("a" has a reference error. It does not state clearly what the rookie should take to the evidence room.)

For question 46, read the following passage and then answer the question based solely on the information provided in the passage.

A uniform is a type of clothing worn by members of an organization while participating in that organization's activity. Modern uniforms are most often worn by armed forces and paramilitary organizations such as police, emergency services, security guards, in some workplaces and schools and by inmates in prisons. In some countries, some other officials also wear uniforms in their duties; such is the case of the Commissioned Corps of the United States Public Health Service or the French prefects. For some public groups, such as police, it is illegal for non-members to wear the uniform. Other uniforms are trade dresses (such as the brown uniforms of UPS).*

46. According to the above passage:

A. Modern uniforms are most often worn by non-military organizations.

B. UPS uniforms are beige.

C. For some public groups, such as police, it is illegal for non-members to wear the uniform.

(This is stated in the next to the last sentence.)

D. Schools must obtain permission for students to wear uniforms.

For question 47, read the following passage and then answer the question based solely on the information provided in the passage.

A vacation or holiday is a leave of absence from a regular occupation, or a specific trip or journey, usually for the purpose of recreation or tourism. People often take a vacation during specific holiday observances, or for specific festivals or celebrations. Vacations are often spent with friends or family.

A person may take a longer break from work, such as a sabbatical, gap year, or career break.

The concept of taking a vacation is a recent invention, and has developed through the last two centuries. Historically, the idea of travel for recreation was a luxury that only wealthy people could afford. In the Puritan culture of early America, taking a break from work for reasons other than weekly observance of the Sabbath was frowned upon. However, the modern concept of vacation was led by a later religious movement encouraging spiritual retreat and recreation. The notion of breaking from work periodically took root among the middle and working class.*

47. Which of the following statements is not supported by the preceding paragraph?

A. A sabbatical is a short break from work.

(A person may take a _longer_ break from work, such as a sabbatical, gap year, or career break.)

B. People often take a vacation during specific holiday observances.

C. Vacations are often spent with friends or family.

D. The concept of taking a vacation is a recent invention.

For questions 48-50, read the following passage and then answer the questions based solely on the information provided in the passage.

The states use different terminology for licenses or permits to carry a concealed firearm, such as a Concealed Handgun License/Permit (CHL/CHP), Concealed Carry Weapons (CCW), Concealed (Defensive/Deadly) Weapon Permit/License (CDWL/CWP/CWL), Concealed Carry Permit/License (CCP/CCL), License to Carry (Firearms) (LTC/LTCF), Carry of Concealed Deadly Weapon license (CCDW), Concealed Pistol License (CPL), etc. Thirteen states use a single permit to regulate the practices of both concealed and open carry of a handgun.

Some states publish statistics indicating how many residents hold permits to carry concealed weapons, and their demographics. For example, Florida has issued 2,031,106 licenses since adopting its law in 1987, and had 843,463 licensed permit holders as of July 31, 2011. It is likely that by December 2012 Florida had reached the milestone of 1 million active licensees within a population of 19 million. Reported permit holders are predominantly male. Some states have reported the number of permit holders increasing over time. "With hard numbers or estimates from all but three of the 49 states that have laws allowing for issuance of carry permits, the U.S. Government Accountability Office reports that there were about 8 million active permits in the United States as of December 31, 2011. That's about a million more than previous estimates by scholars.*

-----

48. Which of the following is not included in the terms used by states to refer to licenses or permits to carry a concealed firearm?

A. License to Carry (Firearms) (LTC/LTCF)

B. Concealed Carry Weapons (CCW)

C. Concealed Pistol License (CPL)

D. Carry of Concealed Non-Deadly Weapon license (CCDW)

(This should read, " Carry of Concealed <u>Deadly</u> Weapon license (CCDW).)

----

49. How many states use a single permit to regulate the practices of both concealed and open carry of a handgun?

A. less than 10

B. thirteen

(Thirteen states use a single permit to regulate the practices of both concealed and open carry of a handgun.)

C. more than 19t

D. fifteen

----

50. According to the preceding passage:

A. For example, Florida has issued <u>2,013,106</u> licenses since adopting its law in 1987, and had 843,463 licensed permit holders as of July 31, 2011.

B. For example, Florida has issued 2,031,106 licenses since adopting its law in 1987, and had 843,463 licensed permit holders as of <u>July 31, 2001</u>.

C. For example, Florida has issued 2,031,106 licenses since adopting its law in 1987, and had 843,463 licensed permit holders as of July 31, 2011.

D. For example, Florida has issued 2,031,106 licenses since adopting its law in <u>1978</u>, and had 843,463 licensed permit holders as of July 31, 2011.

For questions 51-53, read the following passage and then answer the questions based solely on the information provided in the passage.

Crowd control is a public security practice where large crowds are managed to prevent the outbreak of crowd crushes, affray, fights involving drunk and disorderly people or riots. Crowd crushes in particular can cause many hundreds of fatalities. Crowd control can involve privately hired security guards as well as police officers. Crowd control is often used at large, public gatherings like street fairs, music festivals, stadiums and public demonstrations. At some events, security guards and police use metal detectors and sniffer dogs to prevent weapons and drugs being brought into a venue.

Materials such as stanchions, crowd control barriers, fences and decals painted on the ground can be used to direct a crowd. Keeping the crowd comfortable and relaxed is also essential, so things like awnings, cooling fans (in hot weather), and entertainment are sometimes used as well.

Specific products that are used to implement line management and public guidance in high traffic areas include retractable belt systems (which incorporate a stanchion post and the retractable tape) and wall mount systems (also incorporating a retractable belt but are surface mounted). Post and rope systems are also popular, especially in banks and theaters.*

-----

51. According to the above passage:

A. Crowd control only involve police officers.

B. Crowd control does not involve any equipment.

C. Crowd control does not use sniffer dogs if metal detectors are available.

D. Crowd control can involve privately hired security guards as well as police officers.

(This is stated in the first paragraph.)

----

52. Which of the following is not supported by the preceding passage?

A. Crowd often form after sunset.

B. Small crowds are often deadlier than large crowds.

C. Crowd crushes can cause many hundreds of fatalities.

D. Crowd control training must be increased.

----

53. Which of the following statements is supported by the above paragraph?

A. At <u>all</u> events, security guards and police use metal detectors and sniffer dogs to prevent weapons and drugs being brought into a venue.

B. At some events, security guards and police use metal detectors and sniffer dogs to prevent weapons and drugs being <u>removed</u> from a venue.

C. At some events, security guards and police use metal detectors and sniffer dogs to prevent <u>food</u> from being brought into a venue.

D. At some events, security guards and police use metal detectors and sniffer dogs to prevent weapons and drugs being brought into a venue.

(This is the last sentence in the first paragraph.)

For questions 54-55, read the following passage and then answer the questions based solely on the information provided in the passage.

In non-military law enforcement, patrol officers are law enforcement officers assigned to monitor specified geographic areas—that is, to move through their areas at regular intervals looking out for any signs of problems of any kind. They are the officers most commonly encountered by the public, as their duties include responding to calls for service, making arrests, resolving disputes, taking crime reports, and conducting traffic enforcement, and other crime prevention measures. A patrol officer is often the first to arrive on the scene of any incident; what such an officer does or fails to do at the scene can greatly influence the outcome of any subsequent investigation. The patrol officer, as the person who is in the field daily, is often closest to potential crime and may have developed contacts who can provide information.*

-----

54. According to the preceding passage:

A. Special officers are the officers most commonly encountered by the public

B. Detectives are usually the first to arrive on the scene of any incident.

C. Sergeants are the persons who are in the field daily.

D. To patrol means to move through an area at regular intervals looking out for any signs of problems.

(This is stated in the first sentence of the passage.)

----

55. According to the preceding passage, the duties of a patrol officer include all the following, except:

A. taking crime reports

B. officiating at political rallies

C. conducting traffic enforcement

D. resolving disputes

For questions 56-60, read the following passage and then answer the questions based solely on the information provided in the passage.

The United States police rank model is generally quasi-militaristic in structure. Much like the London Metropolitan Police, there are enlisted, non-commissioned, officer, and general officer grades. A uniform system of insignia based on that of the US Army and Marine Corps is used to help identify an officer's seniority.

Chief of police/police commissioner/superintendent/sheriff: The title police commissioner is used mainly by large metropolitan departments, while chief of police is associated with small and medium-sized municipalities; both are typically appointed by a mayor or selected by the city council or commission. In some cities, "commissioner" is the member of the board of officials in charge of the department, while a "chief" is the top uniformed officer answering to the commissioner or commission. In very large departments, such as the New York City Police Department, there may be several non-police officer deputy and assistant commissioners, some of whom outrank the chief of department and others on par with the uniformed chief. There may be a chief of operations who is second in command to the top-ranking chief. In contrast, sheriffs in the United States are usually elected officials, one in each county, who head the sheriff's department (or sheriff's office).

Assistant Chief of Police/Assistant Commissioner/Assistant Superintendent: Only seen in some departments. In New York City, assistant chiefs head borough commands.

Deputy Chief of Police/Deputy Commissioner/Deputy Superintendent/Chief Deputy/undersheriff: The top subordinate of the chief of police, commissioner, superintendent, or sheriff; may or may not have a specific area of responsibility. In some places the undersheriff is the warden of the county jail. The New York City Sheriff's Office has five undersheriffs: each one is responsible for a borough of New York City, with the Sheriff of the City of New York overseeing all of them.

Inspector/commander: Sometimes have an insignia of a single star, analogous to brigadier generals, but in other areas wear a gold or silver eagle, similar to a colonel. "Inspector" is also used as a term for "detective" in the San Francisco Police Department but is two ranks above captain in the NYPD and the Philadelphia Police Department. In the NYPD, Inspectors command divisions, which may be groups of precincts within a borough or specialized branches of the police service.

Colonel: A majority of state police agencies use "colonel" as their senior executive rank, often jointly with a civilian title such as "superintendent," "commissioner" or "director." Conversely, the colonel rank is rarely employed by other agencies, though it is used by the Baltimore Police Department and other Maryland agencies as either an executive or commander-like rank. Colonels generally wear the gold or silver eagle of a colonel, or the oak leaf of a lieutenant colonel, from the U.S. armed forces. Many sheriffs also wear the eagle insignia, and use colonel as an official rank.

Major/deputy inspector: Sometimes have an insignia of a gold or silver oak leaf, similar to a major or lieutenant colonel. In the Baltimore Police Department and Atlanta Police Department majors supervise police stations.*

-----

56. Which of the following is not supported by the preceding passage?

A. Colonels generally wear a gold or silver eagle, or an oak leaf.

B. Major/deputy inspector sometimes have an insignia of a gold or silver oak leaf.

C. Chief of Police sometimes wear five stars.

(This is not stated in the passage.)

D. Inspector/commander sometimes have an insignia of a single star.

----

57. Which of the following statements is not supported by the preceding paragraph?

A. Inspectors/commanders are analogous to brigadier generals.

B. Inspectors/commanders sometimes wear a gold or silver eagle, similar to a colonel.

C. Inspectors command divisions, which may be groups of precincts within a borough or specialized branches of the police service.

D. "Inspector" is also used as a term for "detective" in the New York Police Department.

("Inspector" is also used as a term for "detective" in the San Francisco Police Department.)

----

58. Which of the following statements is not supported by the preceding paragraph?

A. A majority of state police agencies use "colonel" as their senior executive rank.

B. A majority of state police agencies often use "colonel" jointly with a civilian title such as "superintendent," "commissioner" or "director."

C. "Colonel" is used by the Baltimore Police Department and other Maryland agencies as either an executive or commander-like rank.

D. Colonels generally wear the gold or silver eagle of a colonel, or the oak leaf of a lieutenant colonel, patterned from the New York Police Department.

(This should read, "Colonels generally wear the gold or silver eagle of a colonel, or the oak leaf of a lieutenant colonel, from the U.S. armed forces.")

----

59. Which of the following police rank is not discussed in the preceding passage?

A. Inspector

B. Major

C. patrolman

D. Commander

----

60. According to the preceding passage, a uniform system of insignia based on that of the US Army and Marine Corps is used to help identify:

A. age of uniformed person

B. number of commendations

C. number of successful campaigns

D. an officer's seniority.

(A uniform system of insignia based on that of the US Army and Marine Corps is used to help identify an officer's seniority.)

Instructions for Questions 61-105: In the following passages of text, certain words have been deleted and replaced by dashes (one dash for each letter of the word that has been deleted). Using the "contextual clues" in the paragraph, deduce the missing words and record your answers on the answer sheet, as instructed.

Passage 1:

On Tuesday, his first day 61) _ _ the job 62) _ _ Queens County, while Police Officer Jane Sanchez called 63) _ _ _ an ambulance, Kevin administered emergency first aid on 64) _ _ elderly woman who had fainted 65) _ _ _ cut her forehead 66) _ _a court chair.

67) _ _ _ Police Officer assigned to 68) _ _ _ Part, Agnes Milliken, assisted Kevin in lifting the woman from the floor. The ambulance arrived at 11:10 A.M., five minutes after Police Officer Sanchez called 911. The EMT's examined the woman 69) _ _ _ determined that her breathing was unusually labored. They administered oxygen, placed her 70) _ _ a stretcher and rushed 71) _ _ _ to Queens Mercy Hospital, at 45 Brighton Avenue, about twelve blocks away 72) _ _ _ _ the courthouse.

Passage 2:

Police uniforms 73) _ _ many foreign countries 74) _ _ _ the same throughout the country. However, 75) _ _ the United States, the uniforms differ from 76) _ _ _ area to another. 77) _ _ _ _ variety is primarily 78) _ _ _ result of the many decentralized jurisdictions in the 79) _ _ _ _ _ states. Although dissimilar, all uniforms share certain characteristics. All of them 80) _ _ _ designed to present a sharp 81) _ _ _ professional appearance, and they are all designed to make the officers easily identifiable to 82) _ _ _ public and fellow officers.

Passage 3:

Police Officer Trainees receive approximately two months of training at the Police Officers Academy, located at 87 Windham Street. The majority 83) _ _ the training is done in a classroom setting. 84) _ _ the classroom setting, trainees receive instruction 85) _ _ such matters 86) _ _ public relations, criminal statutes, court procedures, first aid 87) _ _ _ crowd control. Training and qualification 88) _ _ the Glock semi-automatic 89) _ _ _ done at 90) _ _ _ firing range located 91) _ _ 12 Leonard Street. Following the academy training, 92) _ _ _ _ _ _ Officer Trainees are assigned 93) _ _ a specific court where they are further trained in the security 94) _ _ _ clerical procedures of that court. Although 95) _ _ _ _ _ _ Officers are primarily responsible 96) _ _ _ security, knowledge of court 97) _ _ _ clerical procedures help them to understand the court process and help them to better serve 98) _ _ _ public.

Passage 4:

The right 99) _ _ appeal a judicial order is 100) _ _ important right for all Americans. During an appeal, both the decision of 101) _ _ _ court and the actual law 102) _ _ _ reviewed. This right to appeal was first recognized during the first dynasty of Babylon, 103) _ _ _ _ King Hammurabi and his governors served as the "appellate courts." Today, almost 104) _ _ _ democratic countries have an appeals process. It is only in dictatorial or oligarchic nations 105) _ _ _ _ the right to appeal is non-existent.

Answer for Questions 61-105:

61. on	76. one	91. at
62. in	77. this	92. police
63. for	78. the	93. to
64. an	79. fifty	94. and
65. and	80. are	95. police
66. on	81. and	96. for
67. the	82. the	97. and
68. the	83. of	98. the
69. and	84. in	99. to
70. on, in	85. in	100. an
71. her	86. as	101. the
72. from	87. and	102. are
73. in	88. in	103. when
74. are	89. are	104. all
75. in	90. the	105. that

CALIFORNIA POST EXAM GUIDE (PELLETB)

Directions for Questions 106-110: In each of the following five questions, there is a number series. For each number series, you are to figure out the pattern in the series and determine what two numbers (represented by dashes) would be the last two numbers in the series.

-----

106)   109 73 105 69...101 65 ___ ___.

A) 97, 61   B) 95, 59   C) 99, 61   D) 97, 63

Answer 106: A (97, 61)

Pattern is two DOUBLE numbers (109 and 73) ALTERNATING and DECREASING by 4 each time.

----

107)   57 72 87 102 117 132 __ __

A) 145, 162   B) 149, 164   C) 143, 162   D) 147, 162

Answer 107: D (147, 162)

Pattern is the number 57 INCREASING by 15 each time the pattern is repeated.

----

108)   1 3 9 27 __ __

A) 81, 242   B) 80, 243   C) 79, 247   D) 81, 244   E) 81, 243

Answer 108: E (81, 243)

Pattern is 1 MULTIPLIED by 3 each time the pattern is repeated (1 X 3 = 3, 3 X 3 = 9, 9 X 3 = 27, 27 X 3 = 81, 81 X 3 = 243).

----

109)   60 64 68 72 76 80 84 88 __ __

A) 92, 96   B) 90, 94   C) 94, 98   D) 91, 95

Answer 109: A (92, 96)

The pattern is the number 60 REPEATED and INCREASED by 4 each time

----

110)   93 84 76 69 63 58 __ __

A) 53, 51   B) 54, 51   C) 54, 52   D) 52, 53   E) 52, 51

Answer 110: B (54, 51)

The pattern is the number 93 DECREASING by a DECREASING number each time the pattern is repeated (93 - 9 = 84, 84 - 8 = 76, 76 - 7 = 69, 69 - 6 = 63, 63 - 5 = 58, 58 - 4 = 54, 54 - 3 = 51).

Directions: For questions 111-115, select the choice containing the word that does not belong in the group of the other three related words.

Question 111:

A. hosiery

B. socks

C. nylons

D. hat (The other 3 words are undergarments. A hat is worn on the head.)

Question 112:

A. jail

B. penitentiary

C. reformatory

D. courtroom (The other 3 words are places where persons are confined. A court is a place for judicial determinations.)

Question 113:

A. bracelet

B. necklace

C. eyeglasses (The other 3 words are jewelry items. Eyeglasses are instruments for increasing one's vision.)

D. pendant

Question 114:

A. church

B. synagogue

C. chapel

D. auditorium (The other 3 words are religious sites. An auditorium may be non-religious.)

Question 115:

A. crook

B. hustler

C. cheater

D. statesman (The other 3 words relate to irregular activities with a negative connotation. A statesman is usually striving for noble aims.)

Question 116

Four screwdrivers used in burglaries were discovered at the suspect's house. One was silver in color and 16 inches long. One was blue and eight inches long. One was red and 12 inches long. One was yellow and fourteen inches long. What color was the third longest screwdriver?

A. blue

B. yellow

C. red

D. silver

(The order, according to length is: 1) blue (8inches), 2) red (12 inches), 3) yellow (14 inches), and 4) silver (16 inches).)

Question 117

Your sergeant gives you five "Complaint Forms" with the following priority numbers:

5293   14275   0698   879   7892

He asks you to organize the forms in ascending priority.

According to the above, the third Complaint Form would be Complaint Form number:

A. 14275   **C. 5293**

B. 0698   D. 879

      The Complaint Forms in Ascending Priority Number Order are as follows:

1) 0698

2) 879

3) 5293

4) 7892

5) 14275

The third complaint number on the list is 5293. Therefore the correct answer is **C) 5293.**

Question 118

Your sergeant gives you five "Requests for Investigation" forms submitted by residents in your precinct. The forms were submitted by the following five persons:

1) Norman Dankin, 2) Leon Cohen, 3) Frank Warden, 4) Michael Forman, 5) Harriet Russfield

He asks you to organize the forms in last name alphabetical order.

According to the above, the fourth "Request for Investigation" form is the one submitted by:

A. Warden, Frank

B. Russfield, Harry

C. Dankin, Norman

D. Forman, Michael

Answer 118

The correct listing in <u>last name alphabetical order</u> is:

1) Cohen, Leon

2) Dankin, Norman

3) Forman, Michael

4) Russfield, Harry

5) Warden, Frank

The fourth name on the list is Russfield, Harry. Therefore, the correct answer is **B. Russfield, Harry**

Directions for Questions 119-120: The following 2 questions are comprised of a series of sentences which are in scrambled order. Select the order of sentences (A, B, C, or D) which most correctly and logically places the sentences in a meaningful, logical, and effective order.

Question 119:

1. If you belong to the exempt group, you must have proper documentation and ID.

2. The announcement also contains a section regarding the exam fee waiver.

3. A combined filing and processing fee is required for this examination.

4. Everyone must pay the fee unless they are exempt by law.

5. The amount of the fee is noted on the examination announcement.

(A) 5-3-4-2-1

(B) 3-5-2-4-1

(C) 3-2-5-4-1

(D) 3-5-2-1-4

Answer 119: (B) 3-5-2-4-1

3. A combined filing and processing fee is required for this examination.

5. The amount of the fee is noted on the examination announcement.

2. The announcement also contains a section regarding the exam fee waiver.

4. Everyone must pay the fee unless they are exempt by law.

1. If you belong to the exempt group, you must have proper documentation and ID.

Question 120 Organize the following four sentences in the best logical order:

1. Among these benefits are dental and optical benefits.

2. If you add to this amount, life insurance and other benefits, the total possible yearly benefit may exceed six or seven thousand dollars per family.

3. Court Assistants and Court Officers are represented by the New York State Court Officer's Association.

4. The combined amount of these two types of benefits may be two thousand dollars per year for each family member.

5. This association provides many quality benefits to its employees.

(A) 3-5-1-4-2

(B) 5-3-4-1-2

(C) 4-5-1-4-2

(D) 3-1-5-4-2

Answer 120: (A) 3-5-1-4-2

3. Court Assistants and Court Officers are represented by the New York State Court Officer's Association.

5. This association provides many quality benefits to its employees.

1. Among these benefits are dental and optical benefits.

4. The combined amount of these two types of benefits may be two thousand dollars per year for each family member.

2. If you add to this amount, life insurance and other benefits, the total possible yearly benefit may exceed six or seven thousand dollars per family.

---

* Wikipedia

Other Civil Service Jobs for Which We Have Exam Prep Books

JOB	Title of Exam Prep Book
New York State Unified Court System	
Court Office Assistant	Court Office Assistant
Senior Court Office Assistant	Court Office Assistant
Court Assistant	Court Office Assistant
New York City	
Police Officer	Police Officer Exam New York City
Police Officer	Police Officer New York City Speed-Prep
Sanitation Worker	Sanitation Worker Exam New York City
Sanitation Worker	Sanitation Worker Exam New York City Speed-Prep
Bridge and Tunnel Police Officer	Bridge and Tunnel Officer Exam New York City
Traffic Enforcement Agent (NYC)	Traffic Enforcement Agent New York City
School Safety Agent (NYC)	School Safety Agent New York City
Florida	
Law Enforcement	Florida Law Enforcement Basic Abilities Test (BAT) Exam Guide
National	
Postal Test	Pass the New Postal Test 473E Second Edition
Postal Test	Postal Test 473E - Speed Study Guide

CALIFORNIA POST EXAM GUIDE (PELLETB)

Books by Angelo Tropea
Non-Fiction

Florida Law Enforcement Basic Abilities Test (BAT) Exam Guide

School Safety Agent New York City

Police Officer Exam New York City
Police Officer Exam New York City Speed-Prep

Sanitation Worker Exam New York City
Sanitation Worker New York City Speed-Study Guide

Bridge and Tunnel Officer Exam New York City

Traffic Enforcement Agent

Court Office Assistant

Pass the New York Notary Public Exam
Pass the New York Notary Public Exam (Questions and Answers)
Notary Public Journal of Notarial Acts
Notary Public Journal 600 Entries
Notary Public Journal Large Entries
Notary Public Journal Two-Page Entries
New York Notary Public Exam Speed-Study Guide
New York Notary Public Reference Guide

California Notary Public Exam

Pass the New Postal Test 2010 Edition
Pass the New Postal Test Second Edition
Postal Test 473E Study Guide

Pass the New Citizenship Test 2012 Edition
Pass the New Citizenship Test Third Edition
Pass the New Citizenship Test Questions and Answers (English, Spanish and Chinese Editions)

Examen de Ciudadania Americana Español Y Inglés

Pass the New Citizenship Test Quick Civics Lessons
Quick Civics Lessons from USICS and Civics Cards for Cut-Out

Canadian Citizenship Test

Goldmine of Baby Names Boys and Girls
Goldmine of Baby Names Boys
Goldmine of Baby Names Girls

Aliens and UFOs: Case Closed
Zombie Pocket Guide

Cruise Fan Tips and Tricks How to Get the Most Out of Your Cruise Adventure
Cruise Fan Cruising With Norwegian
Cruise Fan Bermuda Cruise

NYS Surrogate's Court Procedure Act Vol. 1
NYS Surrogate's Court Procedure Act Vol. 2
NYS Surrogate's Court Procedure Act Vol. 3
NYS Surrogate's Court Procedure Act Vol. 4

Amazing Science News and Facts No. 1

Arizona Civics Test
North Dakota Civics Test
Utah Civics Test
Idaho Civics Test

Fiction
Pinocchio and the Dragons of Martoon (age 12 and up)

NOTES
Additional Spelling Words

<u>NOTES</u>
<u>Additional Vocabulary Words</u>

<u>NOTES</u>

<u>Important Contacts (Names and Telephone Numbers)</u>

<u>OTHER NOTES</u>
<u>Appointments</u>

<u>OTHER NOTES</u>

<u>OTHER NOTES</u>

Made in the USA
San Bernardino,
CA